POVERTY AMONG SCHEDULED CASTES

POVERTY AMONG SCHEDULED CASTES

A Study

By

AROON SHARMA

ANMOL PUBLICATIONS PVT. LTD.
NEW DELHI - 110 002 (INDIA)

ANMOL PUBLICATIONS PVT. LTD.
4374/4B, Ansari Road, Daryaganj
New Delhi - 110 002
Ph.: 23261597, 23278000
Visit us at: www.anmolpublications.com

Poverty Among Scheduled Castes

First Published, 2004

ISBN 81-261-1803-2

PRINTED IN INDIA

Published by J.L. Kumar for Anmol Publications Pvt. Ltd., New Delhi - 110 002 and Printed at Mehra Offset Press, Delhi.

Contents

Preface

Concern for poverty in India has always been universal but after the colonial rules, interest in poverty got momentum at first slowly and then by leaps and bounds. This was due to the realisation that there was nothing divine about poverty, that it was man made, that it was the outcome of retarded development of the forces of production within the limitation of archaic and stagnant relations of production and inadequately rewarded efforts, that it was the symptom of structural crises of present day socio-economic formation and that it could be remedied. This realization acted like a catalyst and fused the aspirations of masses (poor and non-poor) into a definite programme of actions against poverty.

During the early phase of the process of socio-economic transformation of Indian society it was assumed that economic growth by itself would lead to the reduction in the incidence of poverty. However, around seventies it was felt that the benefits of growth have been shared inequitably and therefore, special efforts need to made to supplement the growth process by designing special programmes to cater to the need and development of identified groups. Formulation of programmes to mitigate poverty essentially required knowledge of what are now recognized as enormously complex causes. Empirical identification of these causes is a formidable task because of the conceptual issues involved in defining the many dimensions of poverty, the data constraints in measuring the incidence and econometric problems in estimating relationships between the casual factors and poverty levels. Despite enormous research, these problems have defined a universally accepted solution.

Persistence of these problems inevitably suggests strengthening of efforts to evolve widely accepted framework of research on poverty and the present study is research on poverty and is a modest effort in that direction.

The study is based on the thoughts expressed by large number of social scientists (Sociologists and Economists) in their innumerable writings and originality in any form. The focus of the study (first three chapters) is on the survey of ideas and opinions called from plethora of literature and arranges them in an appropriate manner consistent with the theme of the study. The fourth and fifth chapters are analytical where incidence of poverty among rural scheduled castes in Jammu Tehsil has been calculated. Finally, the main observations and conclusions derived from the study are summed up in chapter six.

Acknowledgements

The present work would not have materialised without the guidance which I received from my teacher Professor O.P. Kotwal, it is he who assiduously chiselled my raw mind and trained and equipped me with the logic and techniques to rationalise the stray ideas. I owe him a deep sense of gratitude for constructive criticism, valuable suggestions and continuous encouragement to accomplish this arduous work. My thanks are also to Prof. R.L. Bhat, Prof. J.R. Panda and Dr. Jasbir Singh for providing me helpful comments, which have contributed to an improvement in the quality of this work. Thanks are also to Sh. Vikram Singh who performed the painstaking job of typing with meticulous care and skill.

—Aroon Sharma

1 Introduction

Historically, there is ample evidence in ancient literature to suggest that the phenomenon and pains of poverty were not unknown to Indians. However, due to the absence of systematic and authentic record of economic conditions in ancient India, opinions among economic historians about the nature of 'material' life enjoyed by the people reflect wide divergence. Historians like M.A. Buch (1922), N.C. Bandhopadhay (1925) and S.K. Das (1929) have opined that economic conditions in ancient India were better than those of their own times. Ghosals made a serious study of the taxation systems of India from the Vedic age to AD 1200 and stated that 'there is little, if any positive evidence, to prove that the burden of taxation in ancient and medieval periods was so heavy as to leave the cultivator a bare margin for subsistence. In another study, "The Agrarian System in Ancient India" Ghoshal states... the glimpses which the observations of the foreign travelers furnish into the actual condition of the people generally indicate a happy and contended peasantry". Following the publication of the full text of *Arthshastra* of Kautilya in 1909, nationalist historians have regarded the ancient period of Indian history as one of considerable prosperity and general contentment. Altekar while analyzing the rural economy of Western India in the early centuries before and after the Christian era asserted, "the people were better off than they are at present". Morris and Stein contended these opinions and observed that the patriotic bias (in the writings of nationalists historians) often resulted in an exaggeration of the self-sufficiency of the early Indian village out of all proportions and greater emphasis on the socially productive aspects of the corporate institutions (Caste included) of the Pre-British India than warranted by available historical evidence. Basu also arrived at the identical conclusions when he emphasized "they (nationalist historians) often tried to cover up the social inequalities characteristic of the early Indian society by vague philosophical platitude. In contrast to the nationalist historians, Bose has tried to show that "all was not well with the ancient economic system and that according to Jataka stories the peasants were exploited by the princes. Observations of R S Sharma (1958) on early Indian feudalism that, "the economic essence of Indian feudalism, like that of the European, lay in the rise of landed intermediaries leading to the enserfment of the peasantry through mounting tax burdens, increasing obligations to perform forced labour and evils of subinfeudation", have lent powerful support to the ideas that peasantry in India during the early period was not free from exploitation. Besides absence of growth factors was noticed in the village communities of ancient India when as early as 1817 James Mill asserted that Indian Society has remained substantially unchanged since its inception. Maity also concluded that as regards the material life of the common people, the Gupta period was not a golden age. For the subsequent period, Pushpa Niyoagi does not find any evidence to prove that the population as a whole was prosperous. L Gopal in one of his studies covering the period AD 700-1200 repeatedly suggests that the common people were far from happy and economically well off.

Opinions regarding economic conditions of the common people during the Mughal period reveal that the prosperity of the nation was, by and large, maintained throughout the rule of Akbar, Jahangir and Shahjahan, but it came to a stand still when in Aurangzeb's reign, the incessant wars and the loss of human life, paralysed agriculture, industry and trade.

According to Hamilton, "in the best days of the Mughal Empire there was indeed a greater degree of prosperity than that of the previous era as also of the days which witnessed the decline of its power. It is widely believed that with the closing years of the reign of Aurangzeb, the economic prosperity of India deteriorated as a natural sequel to the disappearance of peace and order. Thus ensued, observes the historian of Aurangzeb, "a great economic impoverishment of India, not only a decrease of the 'national stock' but also a rapid lowering of mechanical skill and standard of civilization, a disappearing of art and culture over wide tracts of the country". Majumdar and others observed, "it is certain that there was no golden age of opulence for the common people under the Mughals, because though the prices of articles were cheap, their average income was proportionally low or perhaps lower. They did not, however, grovel in misery and smart under discontent as their needs were few and the problems of life were not so complicated as those of the present days".

These historical accounts unmistakenly reveal that India had attained high level of development and the people under normal circumstances were not grinding under poverty and misery. Report of Indian Industrial Commission (1918) has lent support to this view by recording, at a time when the west of Europe, the birth place of the modern industrial systems, was inhabited by uncivilized tribes, India was famous for the wealth of her rulers and for the high artistic skill of her craftsman. And even at a much later period, when merchant adventures from the west made their first appearance in India, the industrial development of this country was at any rate, not inferior to that of the more advanced European nations".

POVERTY DURING BRITISH RULE

With the British dominance over India, parasitical symbioses got established between an advanced trading (later on industrial) nation and a vast agrarian state. In such a symbioses British became strong and prosperous while as India was reduced to the status of weak and poor country. This observation is supported by the terribly poor conditions of nourishment in India as against Britain in 1938-39 as summed up by R C Desai. India's expenditure structure with spending on food was twice as high as in England and about one half on housing indicated palpably low living standard in the country. Further, investigation of the expenditure made by Desai from 1931-32 to 1940-41 at 1938-39 prices showed that living standard in India was declining. During these years the standard of living showed clearly a falling tendency from Rs. 49.15 an average of first four years to Rs. 48.80, the average of his subsequent three years. Absolute misery of industrial workers is also evident as per Desai investigation, which shows that so far as food conditions are concerned prison inmates are better off than the free industrial workers. It is indeed a poor reflection of the Indian economy that an industrial worker in textile industry of Bombay and Madras could manage to have daily consumption of food estimated at 1.54 and 1.37 British pounds respectively as against 1.69 and 1.87 British pounds authorized for Indian inmates in the prisons of Bombay performing light and heavy work respectively. Similarly calorie intake of industrial workers in Bombay and Madras calculated at 2,435 and 2,176 respectively is much less than the calorie intake of Indian prisoners estimated at 2,772 and 3,026 for light and heavy work respectively.

Another proof of growing poverty in India is found in historical records with show that the major industry of the country viz., Agriculture during the British rule was stagnant or even deteriorating, threatening to drive down the population below the Malthusian limit of subsistence. The progressive decline in the value of agricultural output per acre, per worker and per head of population as shown in the table below, lends powerful support to the rampant poverty of masses in rural India.

Table 1.1

Value of Agricultural Output (Rupees)

Years	*Per Acre*			*Per Agricultural Worker*	*Per Head of Population*	
	Average	*Food*	*Non Food*		*Total*	*Food*
1900-05	28	26	38	105	26	20
1910-15	27	25	33	97	27	20
1920-25	26	23	36	93	25	18
1930-35	26	23	38	103	25	17
1940-45	26	22	41	103	22	15

Source: Sinha, J N, *Demographic Trends in Economic History of India*, Ed. Singh V B, p. 116.

It is apparent from Table 1.1 that the value of agricultural output per acre, per worker and per head of population declined from Rs. 28 to Rs. 26, Rs. 105 to Rs. 103 and Rs. 26 to Rs. 22 respectively during 1900-1945. Similarly, the value of foodgrain output per acre and per head of population recorded a fall from Rs. 26 to Rs. 22 and Rs. 20 to Rs. 15 during the same period. These negative trends amply support the contention that poverty was rampant and wide spread in India during the British rule.

Dr. Banerjee has aptly summarized the poverty of Indian masses as follows:

"Ill-fed, ill-clad, ill-lodged, the mass of the people of India leads a dull and dreary existence. The want of proper subsistence impairs the vigour and vitality of the people, who fall easy victims to the attacks of various kinds of disease. Having no reserve to fall back upon in difficult times, they suffer untold misery, whenever there is slight disturbing cause such as drought or failure of the crops. The children of weak and unhealthy parents become weaklings and being themselves ill fed and ill-bred, swell the number of the worthless members of society. Thus, the physical deterioration of the people goes on increasing from generation to generation and with the progress of physical degeneration their moral stamina also tends to become less and less strong".

Many thinkers, while commenting on the economic condition of people during the British rule have convincingly proved that the policies and programmes had inhibitive effect on development and impoverishment of the masses was increasing. Analysing the impact of Permanent Settlement and freedom of trade, Ram Manohar Roy observed:

"In so far as these causes had operated to bring about an increase of wealth, it was confined to landlords and dealers in commodities. What was too evident was the extent of over whelming poverty throughout the country (towns and their immediate vicinity excepted...). It is well known that within a circle of hundred miles in any part of the country, there are to be found very few, if any (besides proprietors of lands) that have the least pretension to wealth or independence, or even the common comforts of life".

He had also come to the conclusion that whatever the system of land tenure—Permanent Settlement or Ryotwari System- "the condition of the cultivators was very miserable". Under the former they were placed at the mercy of the Zamindars avarices and ambition and under the latter, they were subjected to the extortion and intrigues of the surveyors and other government revenue officer's, Joshi and Dadabhai Naoroji examined the profile of a dependent and colonial economy of India with a great deal of perception and sophistication and pointed out that poverty in the country was not only deep but also deepening. Dadabhai Naoroji vibrantly expressed the exploitative aspect of the Indian economy in his characterization of the "two India's" - the two separate worlds that existed in the same country. Dadabhai estimated the per capita income of India at Rs. 20 per annum around the year 1870 and added, "The mass of the people could not get this Rs. 20 as the upper had a larger share than the average, also this Rs. 20 per head included the income or produce of foreign planters or producers in which the interest of the natives did not go further than being mostly common labourers at competitive wages. All the profits of such produce are enjoyed by and carried away from the country by the foreigners". It was against this dismal background that Dadabhai spoke of two India's as follows:

> "In reality there are two Indians - one the prosperous, the other poverty stricken. The prosperous India is the India of the British and other foreigners. They exploit India as officials, capitalists in a variety of ways and carry away enormous wealth to their country. To them, India is, of course, rich and prosperous. The more they can carry away, the richer and more prosperous India is. The second India of the Indians - the poverty stricken India".

Romesh Chander Dutt has sought an explanation from the British rule as to why "the poverty of the Indian people was unparalled in any civilized country" and why "by a moderate calculation, the famines of 1877, 1878 and 1900 had carried off 15 million population, equal to half of England. While discussing the evil economic consequences of Age of Imperialism, Dutt mentioned "It was not gratifying to know that a country possessing a rich and fertile soil, and frugal and industrious population was still subject to recurring famines after a century and half of the British rule". There were no signs of increasing prosperity and greater distress - the recurrence of famines was more frequent and desolation caused greater". Inexorable continuity and increasing intensity of India's poverty was indicated by the low per capita income of 2 pounds as against 48 pounds in Canada and 42 pounds in Great Britain".

Foregoing discussions lead to an inevitable conclusion that under British rule India was getting economically impoverished continuously and therefore, poverty was deepening year after year. Situation on the eve of Independence was thus aptly described as, "India was a rich country but inhabited by poor people".

Poverty in the Post-Independence Period

At the time of Independence, India was a low income country with a near stagnant economy and widespread poverty inherited from a colonial rule. Since, in a low-income country poverty cannot be alleviated without growth, therefore, growth and poverty become concordant. Accordingly during the initial years of development planning, poverty was envisaged to be ameliorated through the spread effects of the various growth oriented programmes and to some extent, through certain special areas and group-based programmes meant for specially less-privileged and depressed sections like scheduled castes and scheduled tribes. With the passage of time it was realized that since the benefits of growth were being shared inequitably, therefore growth by itself was unlikely to reduce inequality and eliminate poverty. It was an inevitable consequence of a predominantly private resource based economy of India, as the better endowed could make a much greater use of the facilities developed in the process of planned development. It was also intriguing to observe that the growth had led to an increase in poverty. Emergence of these trends highlighted the urgency of the programmes aiming not only at accelerated growth but also alleviation of poverty. Hence, around 1970's numerous programmes based on area and/or households approaches were launched to counter poverty of the broadly identified groups of poor such as scheduled castes, tribals, small and marginal farmers and landless labourers.

Poverty, by definition, is a complex phenomenon and such is not amenable to straightforward procedures of identification, aggregation and explanation. The poverty in India has centered around such as; identification; aggregation of poverty; definition of poverty line; nutrition and under nutrition; the deflator to be used to update the nationality specified poverty line and determinants of poverty. A number of studies dealing with poverty problems at the national level are available. However, India, a country of continental size, is characterized by perceptible difference in the levels of living across its space. The inter-regional and intra-regional variations in social and economic development spatial conditions of agricultural development, land tenure systems, demographic structure, urbanization, wage structures, cultural modes and patterns and above all, topography have not received adequate treatment in the poverty studies. The failure at the conceptual and policy levels to fully appreciate the regional dimensions of poverty has rendered the recommended poverty/nutritional norms suspect. Absence of attempts to identify poor households at the regional and sub-regional levels (on the basis of rational socio-economic criteria) have left the gates open to the non-poor families to take advantage of the anti-poverty programmes. Region-specific studies on poverty have as such the potential of providing fresh analytical insights into the depth and magnitude of poverty problems for policy formulation.

Changes in the magnitude of poverty can be appreciated adequately if impact of agrarian transformation and economic development on structural variables like income, consumption and assets are fully captured. The need for poverty studies at the sub-regional levels assumes significance in view of the variation in altitude, climate and living conditions even within the same region.

In the light of the above discussion, the present research work to study the Incidence of poverty among rural scheduled castes - A case study of Jammu Tehsil, assumes significance. Before we embark upon this analysis, it would be desirable to provide the broad features of the area, which has been chosen for the purpose of the present study.

The state of Jammu and Kashmir looks like a crown on the map of India. The state is 640 kms. in length from north to south and 480 kms. from east to west. Its total geographical area is 2, 22, 236 sq. kms. Some part of the state is under the illegal occupation of Pakistan and China. The entire area of the state lies between 32.17" and 37.6" north latitude. And from east to west, the state lies between 73.26" and 80.30" longitude. It is bounded on the north-east by China and the erstwhile USSR and in the west by Pakistan. In the south, the state has its boundary with the states of Punjab and Himachal Pradesh. The state is known for its healthy climate and scenic beauty. On the basis of location, the state occupies a position of unique and strategic importance in the sub-continent.

The total population of the state in 1991 (Due to the disturbed conditions, the 1991 census was not conducted in the state. As such the various figures for 1991 are estimates). Has been estimated to be 77,18,700 with approximately 52 per cent males and 48 per cent females, 76.1 per cent population was living in rural areas and 23.9 per cent in urban areas. The density of population per sq. km. was 76, according to 1991 estimate. The state recorded a decadal population growth of 29.6 percent in 1981, which decreased marginally to 28.9 percent during the decade ending 1991.

Although the state has the population of different religious faiths, but Muslims constitutes the majority of population and are about 64.19 percent of the total population. Hindus are about 32.24 per cent, Sikhs and other religious groups account for 2.4 per cent. Major portion of the state is hilly and altitude from the sea level varies between 1,000 feet to 28,500 feet.

However, the present study is confined to the study of incidence of poverty among rural scheduled castes in Jammu Tehsil of Jammu district only. Jammu Tehsil is one of the five Tehsils of Jammu district of Jammu and Kashmir State.

Jammu district is predominately Hindu majority with 87.37 percent of the population, while as percentage of Muslims, Sikhs and people from other religions are 4.27, 7.64 and 0.72 percent respectively. As far as literacy in the districts is concerned, it was recorded 42.86 percent on account of 1981 census. Whereas male and female literacy rate according to same estimate in Jammu District were estimated to be 52.6 and 32.24 percent respectively. Jammu Tehsil population is 4,30,277 of which 48.09 percent is urban and 51.91 per cent is rural. Scheduled caste's population in the tehsil is 98,193 which is about 22.81 percent whereas rural and urban percentages comes 74.46 and 25.54 respectively. As far as literacy among the scheduled caste is concerned, it was recorded 26 percent. On account of 1981 census, whereas male and female literacy rate according to the same estimates in Jammu Tehsil were estimated to be 19.69 percent and 7.01 percent respectively. The total number of inhabited villages in the Jammu Tehsil is 315 and total area is 90695.51 hectares of which 43.28 percent is the cultivable area to the total area [DOS, 1994-95, J&K Govt.].

Jammu Tehsil experience tropical heat and the climatic conditions are very similar to the plains of Punjab. The average temperature varies between 3 - 4°C in December - January to a maximum of 43 - 47°C in May - June. The average rainfall in the tehsil ranges between 60 and 70 inches. For the district as a whole, January is the coldest and June is the hottest month of the year.

Due to the rural domination, Agriculture is the main occupation of the people of Jammu as well as Jammu and Kashmir State Majority of the rural workers of Jammu Tehsil are engaged in agriculture and draw their subsistence directly or indirectly from this sector. Even those engaged in industries; also depend on agriculture for food and raw materials. So the development of agriculture has its direct impact on the economy of the tehsil and its people.

The areas, which receive an annual rainfall of 150 cm. or above, do not require artificial irrigation. The state does not receive rainfall throughout the year and sometimes it is quite insufficient. Rainfall in the state is neither uniform nor certain. It varies from place to place. In Jammu Tehsil, temperature conditions favour cultivation of crops throughout the year. The rainy season provides sufficient water from July to September. In winter, this tehsil also receives several showers of rain. The remaining months of the year are dry. In order to ensure the availability of water in the remaining months, different sources of irrigation in the tehsil are canal, tube wells, lift irrigation system and springs in some parts of hilly areas. About 35 percent of the total cultivable land is irrigated by these sources.

Cropping pattern tells us about the type of crops grown and their respective acreage. The cropping pattern in a country, in a state or in a region normally changes with the changes in agricultural prices, government policies, input costs of various crops and other related factors. In Jammu Tehsil, the cropping pattern has been biased in favour of conventional and subsistence food crops. In the area under study, during Rabi seasons - wheat, oil seeds, pulses, potatoes etc. are mainly grown whereas paddy, maize, oil seeds, pulses are the main Kharief crops. Wheat, paddy and maize are the major crops of Jammu Tehsil.

2

Concept and Incidence of Poverty: A Review

Human race has lived for ages in a scarcity economy. Co-existence of poverty and opulence both in time and space is the logical consequence of the operations of such as economy. Persistence and perpetuation of poverty was even considered necessary for maximum good of a minimum number of people. Thomas Mun upheld the view that "penury and want do make a people wise and industrious". Arthur Young asserted that "everyone but an idiot knows that the lower classes must be kept poor or they will never be industrious". John Law argued, "labourers were to blame for recurring high prices because of their 'insufferable' habits of idleness contracted when food was cheap". David Hume also supported this belief by stating that in "years of scarcity, if it be not extreme, the poor labour more and really live better than in years of great plenty when they indulge themselves in idleness and idiocy" (Schultz, TW). Poverty is also romanticized by suggesting that a poor who lives in the present develops a capacity for spontaneity, for the enjoyment of the sensual for the indulgence of impulse, which is often blunted in the middle class future-oriented person.

Another variant of the Doctrine of the Utility of the poverty rests on the belief that there are subcultures in our society composed of people who prefer to be poor. Kenneth Boulding states that "a certain amount of the poverty of the hill billy or of the subsistence farmer and ever perhaps of the urban slum dweller and of the buon, involves the rejection of the psychological cost of getting rich and a rejection of the middle-class way of life rather than the inability to find opportunities" (Boulding, KE).

Carcinogenic consequences of poverty have emphasized that it is easier to praise poverty than to live in it. The doctrine of the Disutility of Poverty exhorts that social preferences based on human values are such that a reduction in poverty most certainly will enhance satisfactions. Poverty, thus, is socially undesirable and must therefore be banished. Smolensky while stressing on the externality characteristic of poverty laid greater emphasis on the social consequence of poverty for the community than on the needs of the poor. He suggested that the poverty line should serve as an index of the disutility to the community of the persistence of poverty". In the same vein Rein expressed the view that people must not be allowed to become so poor that they offend or are hurtful to society. It is not so much the misery and plight of the poor but the discomfort and the cost of the community, which is crucial to this view of poverty. We have a problem of poverty to the extent that the low income creates problems for those who are not poor. Poverty then consists of social problems correlated with low income. Hence only when income conditioned problems are randomized can poverty be eliminated. To improve the level of the poor without reducing disutility to the rest of the community is insufficient. Underlying theme in the writings of Titmus, considered poverty as more than the lack of income. He opined "we cannot delineate the new frontiers of poverty unless we take account of the changing agents and characteristics of inequality"(Titmus, R). Townsend contended that the description, analysis and explanation of poverty in any country must proceed within the context of a general theory of stratification as applied to the social systems and sub-systems on a continuum ranging from the household or family at one extreme through local communities and national societies at the other. Thus, according to him "poverty must be regarded as a general form of relative deprivation which is the effect of misdistribution of resources viz; cash income, capital assets and three systems of benefits in kind employment benefits, public social service benefits and private benefits" (Townsend Peter).

These views relate concept of poverty to the non-poor and do not consider poverty as a characteristic of the poor. Conceptualization of poverty must highlight the problems confronting the poor (such as squalar disease, deprivation etc.) rather than its causes and consequences. It is thus contended that the concept of poverty must concern with the conditions of the poor.

Concept of Poverty

Two radically different approaches to the definition of poverty have been advanced; on the one hand, 'culture of poverty' and on the other, 'economic definition'. The focus of cultural concept of poverty is on the internal attitudes and behaviour patterns of the poor with respect to the set of circumstances while as the economic concept highlights the external circumstances that condition a person's behaviour towards economic transactions.

(A) CULTURE OF POVERTY

On the leading protagonists of this view, Oscar Lewis defines 'culture of poverty' as permanent way of life that develops among the poor people under the following set of conditions :

1. a cash economy, wage labour and production for profit.
2. a persistently high rate of unemployment and under employment for unskilled labour.
3. low wages.
4. the failure to provide social, political and economic organization either on a voluntary basis or by

government imposition, for the low income population.

5. the existence of a bilateral kinship system rather than unilateral one; and finally.
6. the existence in the dominant class a set of values that stress the accumulation of wealth and property, the possibility of upward mobility and thrift and that explains low economic status as the result of personal inadequacy or inferiority.

Lewis described the culture of poverty in terms of some seventy interrelated social, economic and psychological traits. In the tradition of qualitative characterization of poverty, Rossi and Blum have identified as the following critical of the poor.

1. Labour-force Participation

Long periods of unemployment and/or intermittent employment. Public assistance is frequently a major source of income for extended periods.

2. Family and Interpersonal Relations

High rates of marital instability (desertion, divorce, separation), high incidence of households headed by females, high rates of illegitimacy, unstable and superficial interpersonal relationships characterized by considerable suspicion of persons outside the immediate household.

3. Community Characteristics

Residential areas with very poorly developed voluntary associations and low levels of participation in such local voluntary associations exist.

4. Relationship to Large Society

Little interest in or knowledge of the large society and its events; some degree of alienation from the larger society.

5. Value Orientations

A sense of helplessness and low sense of personnel efficacy, dogmatism and authoritarianism in political ideology, fundamentalist religious views with some strong inclinations towards belief in magical practices. Low 'need achievement' and low levels of aspiration for the self.

Lewis held the view that the culture of poverty is not only sustained by external environment-poverty - but also by internal systems of values and performances and inter personnel relationships that have a validity and life of their own and that are capable of persisting well after the external circumstances have been modified or changed altogether. Poor people react to change in terms of prior values and behaviour patterns and adopt only those changes that are congruent with their culture. Poverty creates pathologies (adaptation to deprivation degradation and destitution) that block the ability to adopt to non-pathological situations (Lewis, Hylan). The culture of poverty is an adaptation and a reaction of the poor to their marginal position in a class stratified, highly individuated capitalistic society. It represents an effort to cope with feelings of helplessness and despair, which develop from the realization of the improbability of achieving success it, terms of values and goals of the larger society. It is not only an adaptation to a set of objective conditions of the larger society but also tends to perpetuate itself from generation to generation. In fact intergenerational transmission of the characteristics of culture of poverty is near inevitability. At this point a question is begged, should the 'culture of poverty' refer only to those socio-cultural-psychological traits and behaviour patterns of the poor that negate the upward movement or should it also include those persisting cultural patterns among the affluent that deliberately keep their fellow citizens poor. Viewed in this perspective. Lewis concept of 'Culture of Poverty' is less concerned with culture than with situational factors that bring about culture, it is less a culture of poverty than sociology of the underclass (Gans, Herbert).

Basically, characteristics of the poor are situation rather than cultural "POVERTY" writes Otis Dudley Duncan, "is not a trait but a condition".

Conceptualization of poverty along the cultural traits defies its measurement and therefore, whether or not culture of poverty is growing or shrinking remains unanswered. Similarly, whether or not the poor are better off or worse than in past remains unexplained. Thus, the concept of poverty must be lucid and should reflect a single definable, quantifiable characteristic that all poor families and only poor families possess.

(B) DEFINITION OF POVERTY

Not with standing the probing of economists in the factors that account for poverty and their interest in poverty alleviation programme, there is no integrated body of economic knowledge to get at the perfect understanding about poverty. Consequently, unlike economic stability and growth, poverty for want of a theory is lost in economies (Schultz, T W). Economists like Smith, Ricardo, Mathus, Mill, Marx, Marshall and Pigou have made occasional excursions into the area of poverty, but modern economists have not found poverty to their analytical taste. Discontentment with 'trickle down theory' to help alleviate poverty in a reasonable period and growing disutility of poverty to poor and non-poor have urged economists in recent years to chisel their tools and techniques to identify, measure and eradicate poverty.

The central point of economic (objective) definition of poverty is that it is a property of the individual's situation rather than a characteristic of the individual or of his pattern of behaviour. Economists while agree that a meaningful concept of poverty should possess the attribute of measurability objectivity, comparability and sensitivity to changes, yet they have not evolved an universally accepted concept of poverty. Hence conceptualization of poverty depends on the approach adopted by the researcher to the phenomenon of poverty. Most of the research on poverty has adopted either of the following approaches to defining poverty.

1. Subsistence Approach

This approach to define poverty objectively refers to a condition of acute physical want-starvation, near starvation, or a diet-conducive to malnutrition and disease, lack of clothing or shelter necessary for protection from inclement elements, absence of minimal medical service. Poverty thus, is a situation, which denies minimum food and shelter necessary to maintain/sustain life. Rountree perhaps was the first researcher to define poverty in subsistence terms he opined:

> "My primary poverty line represented the minimum sum on which physical efficiency could be maintained. It was a standard of bare subsistence rather than living. In calculating it, the utmost economy was practiced. Nothing must be bought but that which is absolutely necessary for the maintenance of physical health and what is bought must be the plainest and most economic description" (Rountree, BS).

It is thus possible to determine the norm of bare subsistence if human passions for frivolity are ruthlessly curbed. In the event of failure to regulate the spending behaviour of the consumer unit, it will move into a state of secondary poverty (Rountree, B S). Secondary poverty exists when income is adequate to maintain a subsistence level, but the family fails to spend its income to purchase the necessities to sustain life and health. Gadgil states "poverty is nothing but standard of living below a certain minimum. Following Rountrees work (1901) he distinguishes between two types of poverty:

a) Primary poverty resulting from inadequate income, and

b) Secondary poverty caused by an "ignorant and careless house keeping and other improvident expenditure" of an adequate income.

In the same wake Martin Rein describes poverty as lack of the income needed to acquire the minimum necessities of life. It is while true that starvation is the most telling aspect of poverty, but it should not be taken to mean actually dying of lack of food; rather badly fed and clothed, wretchedly housed and miserable in general.

Conceptualization of 'minimum necessities of life' in an objective manner confronts issues that are hard to resolve, for the needs, which are basic, conditioned not only by the physical and climatic environment but also by social structure and culture. Requirement of 'minimum necessities' to sustain and procreate life also vary with age, sex, vocation and other attributes of the consuming unit therefore standardization of a 'basket of necessities' needed to alleviate poverty is a difficult preposition. It is thus, convenient to perceive that individuals with identical levels of income may have different 'standards of living'. Similarly, families with different levels of income living in varying set of conditions situations may not enjoy different 'standard of living'. Hence, the dividing line between the 'poor' and 'non-poor' is neither permanent nor uniform, but changes both in space and time.

Notwithstanding these limitations, it is possible to lay a foundation for the economic definition of poverty with held of the Neo-Classical model of economic choice. According to this model every decision-making unit (individual/family) on the basis of his tastes, values and knowledge (assumed constant) has a 'system of preferences' among the given objects say necessities and luxuries. Given the system of preferences, his 'choice' is constrained by the levels of income, as is show with the help of indifference Curve analysis (Fig. 1).

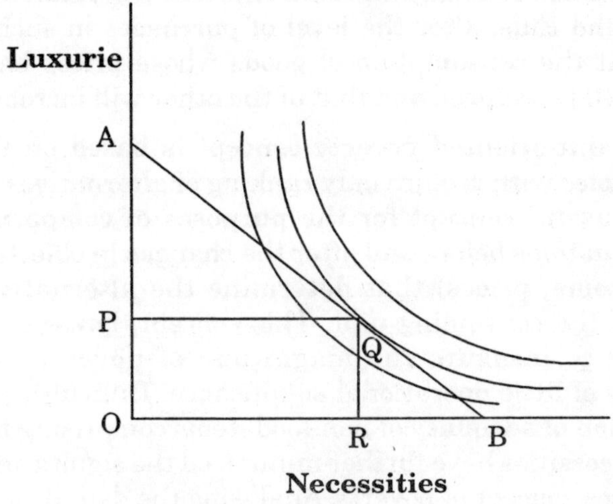

Fig. 1

The model indicates that the consuming unit with preferences indicated by the indifference curves confronted with a budget limit and prices would choose to consume necessities at the rate R and luxuries at rate P. The model makes the distinction between preferences and constraints and limits the concept of poverty to the relatively objective constraint side of the problem. The ex-post facto choices reflect both preferences and constraints, but poverty is associated with severe construction of the choice imposed by the lower level of income. This definition of poverty is focused on the means for pursuit of betterment and argues that anyone with sufficient command over goods and services (Income) will move to higher indifference curve and will be better off.

It must, however, be remembered that the external factors such as income and prices are subjected to variation. An increase in income would shift the constraint outward in a parallel manner and would lead to increased purchases of both commodities. A change in relative prices will rotate the constraint and thus, alter the level of purchases in such a manner that the consumption of goods whose prices have increased will be reduced and that of the other will increase.

Constraint-oriented poverty concept is based on the theory of choice with require only ranking of alternatives. It is, thus, a useful concept for the purposes of comparing different situations before and after the changes in objective factors (income, prices) that determine the alternatives available to the consuming unit. This concept, however, is not helpful to measure the magnitude of poverty and therefore, is of little operational significance. Difficulties in the estimation of adequacy of non-food items comprising the basket of necessities have further minimized the significance of subsistence concept of poverty. Analysing the definition of poverty, Luck opined:

> "The wants to be considered here are recognized biological necessities-food and drink. Little will be said about housing. The need for shelter varies according to locale and to social custom, it cannot be accurately measured. Fuel is essential for survival in a cold environment, but this too is a regional and variable necessity. A similar consideration applies to clothing. The conventional biological definition of necessity — excludes, except for reproduction, almost everything except food and water. "In the light of foregoing observations, it is perhaps reasonable to conclude that except food, there is an absence of standard of adequacy for essentials of living".

2. Nutritional Criteria of Defining Poverty

Another variant of biological concept of poverty is nutritional inadequacy. This definition implies a nutritional criterion of the minimum calorie intake below, which there is under nutrition and also some 'norm' for determining the minimum cost of an adequate diet. The criteria of determining minimum nutritional requirements for calories and other essential nutrients do not itself have an unambiguous connotation in quantitative terms. Not only has it undergone change with time, but there has also been some dispute about using the average requirement, based on the reference individual and equivalences for and as the criterion to be used for judging the nutritional status of an entire population. Further, "even with food", Orshansky acknowledge, "social conscience and custom dictates that there be not only sufficient quantity but sufficient variety to meet recommended nutritional goals and confirm to customary eating patterns. Calories alone will not be enough. Yet food alone provides the best basis for measuring minimum requirements". Orshansky goes on to advocate that the food plan should be developed on the "basis of an acceptable trade-off between nutritional standards and consumption patterns.

There is, thus, a lack of agreement on the criteria of nutritional adequacy, for the per capita requirements of calories depends upon such diverse factors as age, sex, body weight and occupation etc. of the consuming unit. The first and second Food and Agriculture Organization (FAO) committee on requirements suggested on energy expenditure per day of 3,200 calories for the reference man and 2,300 calories for the reference woman. The third FAO Committee reduced these figures to 3,000 and 2,200 calories in 1977. Similarly in case of India the recommended calorie intake, first formulation in 1944 was revised in 1958 and then again in 1968 and in 1980 and is now placed at 2,400 calories for man and 1900 calories for woman per day (Rao, V K R V). The joint expert group of the FAO/WHO has recommended a minimum of 2,223 calories per capita per day for the people in Asia and Far East. Dandekar and Rath have agreed for 2,250 calories as the irreducible minimum requirement or cut-off point.

Goven and Dixon have worked out the average energy requirement for the Indian population at 1965-kilo calories per day. Planning Commission, Government of India recommends 2,400 calories per person per day for rural India and 2,100 calories for urban areas, which works out to 2,350 calories for the population as a whole including both its urban and rural segments. Acharya places the per capita requirements at 2,124 calories per day. Sukhatme suggests the cut-off point for Indian population at 2,200 calories per head per day. The research and planning division of ECAFE Secretariat assumes that for India, the minimum need for calorie intake is 2500 plus 80 protein units. Persual of the studies on poverty conducted in India indicates that most of them assume the calorie requirements at 2,250 per capita per day; which are to be obtained from the wide range of cereals, pulses, fruits, vegetables, meat, eggs, milk etc.

It is apparent from the foregoing discussion that these two biological attributes of poverty (subsistence and nutritional) converge on the minimum food requirement criteria, which in itself is faulty and defective. Problems associated with the subsistence concept of poverty are sought to be minimized by defining "necessities" as products on which the proportion of income expended declines as income rises, "luxuries" as products on which expenditure rises as income rises. Problems pertaining to the estimation of minimum requirement of 'non-food' items comprising the consumption basket are solved by converting expenditure for food into total expenditure with the help of following relationship:

Te = Fe. E

Where

Te = Cost of total consumption of the household.

Fe = Expenditure for a minimum food basket.

E = Size of angles co-efficient.

Alternatively, expenditure on individual 'non-food' items is estimated with the help of the principle of "income elasticity of demand". For example, in case of clothing, as income of the family rises, it reaches a critical point where the number of additional units purchased declines and the price paid per unit increases. This point is defined as the 'clothing poverty line'. Similarly, poverty lines or the cut-off points with respect to other items of the consumption basket are determined and then these points are pooled to draw the poverty line.

A nutritional criterion of poverty measurement is also subject to various limitations. There is no single 'subsistence' level, which can be adopted for the estimation of the poverty line. There is no one level of food intake required for subsistence, but rather a broad range where physical efficiency declines with a falling intake of calories and proteins. Further, even if nutritional requirements are determined in terms of calories, proteins, etc., there would be problems arising from the disparity between expert judgement and actual consumption behaviour, not only due to the lack of dietary knowledge and uneconomic ways of expenditure by the poor families on food purchasing but also due to the eating habits which are profoundly influenced by culture and social traditions and conventions. In case of non-food items, there is even greater degree of arbitrariness, because minimum needs norms and the other factors change from region to region due to the climatic and social factors. Dantwala has also opined that a uniform 'norm' either in terms of the food basket, which would provide minimum subsistence or its equivalent in money terms (due to price variations) would not be appropriate. Issues pertaining to the estimation of nutritional requirements with respect to the nature and degree of activity particularly the leisure activity have defied precise and flawless solutions.

Despite these shortcomings of the biological (nutritional aspect) concept of poverty, malnutrition constitutes core of poverty. Attempts to dismiss this approach to define poverty are fraught with the possibility of adopting standards or criteria, which do not highlight the central issue in the concept of poverty.

3. The inequality Approach

This approach stresses that inequality and poverty are congruent and hence co-terminus with each other. The bottom 10,15 or more percent of population on the income scale is poor and therefore, egalitarian distribution of income is both a necessary and sufficient condition for alleviation of poverty. Kuznet's generalization based on inter-national cross-section and time series evidence that income tends to be more unequally distributed in the developing (poor) economies than in those which have attained some degree of maturity lends support to this approach. Earlier economists like Adam Smith, JS Mill and Alfred Marshall also recognized that the distribution of income affects poverty and observed, "Although poverty was defined in absolute terms, each generations 'poor' are mainly these significantly below the average income" level.

The stratification approach necessitates the extension of the concept of poverty beyond the narrow limits of income and views the poor as those who are lagging behind relatively to others in society. Miller and Roby consider poverty and inequality as identical and support this contention by concluding:

"In the spongy openness of the affluent society, poverty becomes not only a shorthand expression for inequality but a truncated phrase for the many ways in which the poor are different in society. Lasting the issues of poverty in terms of stratification leads to regarding poverty as an issue of inequality. In this approach we move away from efforts to measure poverty lines with pseudo-scientific accuracy instead we look at the nature and size of the differences between the bottom 20 or 10 percent and the rest of society. Our concern becomes one of narrowing the differences between those at the bottom and the better off in each stratification dimension. In casting of the issues of poverty in terms of stratification, we do not wish to imply that the poor are a fixed homogeneous group that shares a common outlook. Rather, we see the poor as those who lay behind the rest of society in terms of one or more dimensions of life – A stratification approach implies that economic goals are not the only important objectives. The multi-dimensional concerns of stratification force attention to the non-economic aspects of inequality–The stratification perspective leads us to see that in dealing with poverty, we are dealing with the quality of life of individuals and not just their economic position. This means that not only individuals relationship to government but the quality of relationships among people in society are important" [Beckar, G S; Chiswick, BR].

"Three broad concepts of poverty can be identified. Poverty may be regarded as subsistence, inequality or externality. Subsistence is concerned with the minimum of provision needed to maintain health and working capacity. Its terms of reference are the capacity to survive and to maintain physical efficiency. Inequality is concerned with the relative position of income groups to each other. Poverty cannot be, understood by isolating the poor and treating them as a special group. Society is seen as a series of stratified income layers and poverty is concerned with how the bottom layers fare relative to the rest of the society. Hence, the concept of poverty must be seen in the context of society as a whole. The study of the poor then depends on an understanding of the level of living of the rich, since it is these conditions relative to each other that are critical in the conception of inequality. To understand the poor we must then study the affluent. Externality is concerned with the social consequences of poverty for the rest of society rather than in terms of the needs of the poor. The poverty line should serve 'as an index of the disutility to the community of the persistence of poverty" [Rein, Martin].

Bhatty (1974) stated that both absolute and relative poverty are closely aligned to inequality in income distribution. Relative poverty arises entirely as a consequence of an unequal distribution of income irrespective of what the income level, or the corresponding state of deprivation, of the people at the bottom end of the income scale might be. Absolute poverty on the other hand expresses a collective view as deprivation in its somewhat physical manifestation.

There is much to commend about this approach but to establish equivalence between inequality and poverty would be injudicious. Inequality and poverty although are not unrelated to each other, but they do not subsume each other. Redistribution of income in favour of low-income category must, other things remaining the same, reduce inequality, but it may leave the perception of poverty unaltered. Similarly, a widespread reduction in the level of income may leaves the pattern of income distribution and hence degree of inequality unchanged but will, most certainly cause intensification of poverty due to increase in hardship, misery and disease. Further, this approach is inappropriate for it ignores hunger and starvation, the two most important parameters of commonly understood concept of poverty. Thus, poverty is more than inequality, the poor undoubtedly receive an unequal share of resources, therefore, it must be related to the larger explanation of social inequality in general.

4. Relative Deprivation Approach

Deprivation is a multi-dimensional concept and connotes objectively evident conditions wherein people lack the basic elements to life and well being. Since, unmet needs can be defined satisfactorily only in terms relative to the society in which they are found, therefore, needs which are basic can be shown to be relative. Accordingly Townsend suggests that "poverty must be regarded as a general form of relative deprivation which is the effect of the misdistribution of resources and that section of the population whose resources are so depressed from the mean as to be deprived of enjoying the benefits and participating in the activities which are customary in that society can be said to be in poverty. This is not the same thing as saying that the poor are the 10 percent or 20 percent in every society with the least resources. Townsend's concept of deprivation is much broader than the one represented on the score of per capita income or expenditure scale. He argues that, "possession by individual and families of relatively low resources does not automatically mean that they are in poverty, but only if they are thereby unable to have the types of diets, participate in activities and have the living conditions and amenities which are customary in that society". Dorothy Wedderburn stated that "individual, families and groups in the population can be said to be in poverty when they lack the resources to obtain the types of diets, participate in the activities and have the living conditions and amenities which are customary or are at least widely encouraged or approved in the societies to which they belong. Their resources are so seriously below those commanded by the average individual or family that they are in effect, excluded from ordinary living patterns, customs and activities". Atkinson states that, "a poverty line to separate deprivation from comforts is necessarily drawn in relation to social conventions and the customary living standards of a particular society and in this way somebody in the United States may be adjudged poor even through he has higher income than the average person in India".

Thus, the concept of deprivation refers not only to the lack of resources whereby an average life style is denied to the individuals and families but also to the 'feeling' of deprivation for want of opportunities to catch up with the better privileged sections of society. Feeling of deprivation is also related to the expectations of individual's families. It is argued that "conditions of deprivation" are of greater usage for it can be applied objectively to describe situations where people possess less of some desired attributes be it income, favourable employment or power, than do others" [Townsend, Peter].

Since, the choice regarding conditions of deprivation is conditional by the individuals valuation (element of subjectively is involved) therefore, feeling of deprivation cannot easily be dissociated from the 'conditions' of deprivation. Thus, determination of 'conditions' objectively inevitably requires 'concrete' understanding of feelings. In this context, Peter Townsend has aptly pointed out the importance of the "endeavor to define the style of living which is generally shared or approved in each society and find whether there is a point in the scale of distribution of resources below which families find it necessarily difficult to share in the customs, activities and diets comprising that style of living". Further, the 'reference group' selected for comparison also influences 'feelings of deprivation'. This poses a grave problem for 'comparison' is not independent of communities' political activity, information flow and changing perceptions of individuals which in turn effect individuals expectations and his views about the fair share in the national cake and his right to share it, all this in turn influence the 'feeling of deprivation'. In this regard Dantwala opined that "Judging on the basis of U. S. official 'norm' for poverty in 1970, probably 99 per cent of India's population could be said to be living in poverty . . . therefore, frame of reference for identification and measurement of poverty has to be 'nation-rational".

Concept of 'relative deprivation' is useful for the understanding of poverty as a socio-economic and non-political phenomenon but it cannot form the basis of conceptualization of poverty for, absolute deprivation (starvation, malnutrition, hardship etc.) constitute the central idea of poverty. At best "the approach of relative deprivation supplements rather than supplants the analysis of poverty in terms of absolute dis-possession" [Sen, AK].

5. A Policy Definition

All societies abhor the persistence of poverty and hence adopt their own 'norms' or 'standards' to identify, measure and formulate programmes for its alleviation:

"If society believes that the people should not be

permitted to die of starvation or exposure, then it will define poverty as the lack of minimum food and shelter necessary to maintain life. If society feels some responsibilities for providing to all persons an established measure of well being beyond mere existence, for example, good physical health, then it will add to its list of necessities the resources required to prevent or cure sickness. At any given time a policy definition reflects a balancing of community capabilities and desires. In low-income societies the community finds it impossible to worry much beyond physical survival. Other societies, more able to support their dependent citizens, begin to consider the effects that pauperism will have on the poor and non-poor alike" [Planning Commission, GOI].

One of the basic problems confronting this approach relates to the nexus between the policy and the polity and invokes an unending debate on "what should be done" and "what could be done" to eliminate poverty. Policy formulation inevitably involves "assessment of feasibilities" but the unfeasibility of elimination of specific deprivation must not be construed as absence of deprivation. Inescapable poverty is still poverty. Further, nature and content of state policy are influenced by political considerations and may reflect aside from feasibility considerations, objectives other than poverty eradication.

Conclusion

It is held that characteristics of the poor are situational rather than cultural. Culture as criteria to define poverty refers to the consequences of poverty for; poverty is not a trait but a condition. Deprivation is, indeed, a central point in the concept of poverty but 'relative' deprivation explains poverty in-appropriately for it ignores absolute dispossession as a 'core' of poverty. Emphasis to consider poverty as an issue in inequality is misplaced. Poverty and inequality are related to each other but neither subsumes the other. Policy definition of poverty displays political overtones and concedes a part of poverty because it is unfeasible to eliminate it. Widely criticized biological approach to define poverty needs to be refined rather than rejected for, it focuses, attention on the critical issues of poverty-hunger and starvation. This approach with suitable refinements constitutes the basis of most of the studies of poverty aiming at its measurement and prescription of policies for its eradication.

SECTION - II

1. Lydall's Estimates of Income Distribution

In one of his pioneering studies, F.H. Lydall calculated the income distribution pattern for the year 1955-56 by utilizing the data obtained from income tax records and the NSS data on consumption expenditure (Lydall, 1960). His findings reveal that per capita income of 86 per cent of the households was less than 360 (at current prices) per annum and of these, 69 per cent had an annual per capita income of Rs. 240 (at current prices) or less. He also pointed out that per capita income of about 72 per cent people was less than the national average of 255 (at current prices) and the remaining 28 per cent people concerned 51 per cent of the national income while the poorest 25 per cent of the population accounted for only 9.5 per cent of the national income. He also noted that top 10 per cent households had garnered 34 per cent of country's national incomes.

2. Estimates of Iyengar and Mukherjee

N.S. Iyengar and M.M. Mukherjee jointly worked out the distribution of personal household income for the years 1952-53, 1953-54 and 1956-57 (1961). They did not consider the use of income tax data appropriate to estimate personal income distribution and therefore, adopted NSS data pertaining to the size distribution of total consumer expenditure and aggregate saving estimates calculated by the Reserve Bank of India for their analysis. Their chief findings are summarized in Table 2.1.

It is clear from Table 2.1 that top 5 per cent of the household recorded an increase in the share of personal income from 14 per cent in 1952-53 to 17.5 per cent in 1956-75. Likewise the shares of top 10 per cent and bottom 20 percent rose from 24 per cent to 25 per cent and from 7.5 per cent to 8.5 per cent respectively during the corresponding period. It is thus obvious that improvement in the shares of these fractile groups was at the cost of middle-income group.

Table 2.1

Estimates of Personal Income Distribution

Fractile Group (P.C. of Household)	*Iyengar and Mukherjee's Estimates*		
	1952-53	*1953-54*	*1954-55*
95-100	14.0	14.0	17.5
90-100	24.0	23.0	25.0
0-20	7.5	8.0	8.5

Source: Iyengar and Mukherjee (1961).

3 Estimates of the Reserve Bank of India

The study of the Reserve Bank of India on Income distribution covered a three-year period from 1953-54 to 1956-57(RBI, 1962). It was based on all the available data but did not use the absolute magnitudes of the NSS data and Income Tax data; instead it applied the proportions revealed in these data to the households and incomes independently. The study did not use NSS data for a single year rather; it used two-year averages beginning from 1953-54. The main conclusions of the study are presented in the Table 2.2.

Table 2.2

Estimates of the Income Distribution (R.B.I. Study)

Fractile Group of P.C. of Household	*Rural*	*Urban*	*Total*
95-100	17	26	20
90-95	25	37	28
50-90	44	38	44
0-20	9	7	8

Source: R.B.I. *'Distribution of Income in the Indian Economy', 1953-54 to 1956-57.* Reserve Bank of India, September 1962.

Table 2.2 reveals that the top 5 per cent of the household commanded a share of 20 per cent in the national income while as their share was 17 per cent and 26 per cent in rural and urban areas respectively. It also shows that the bottom 20 per cent of the households accounted for 8 per cent of the national income as against 9 per cent and 7 per cent in the rural and urban sectors respectively. Thus, the study revealed that income distribution was more skewed in the urban than in the rural sector.

4. Estimates of National Council of Applied Economic Research

The National Council of Applied Economic Research analysed the problem of income distribution without using the NSS and income tax data. Rather, it is independently carried out an urban household survey of income and saving in 1960 and a rural household survey of income and savings in 1962. Later it conducted another All India Consumer Expenditure Survey in 1964-65. The results of these surveys are summarized in Table 2.3 & 2.4.

Table 2.3

Estimates of Income Distribution (1960) NCAER

Fractile Group	*P.C. of Household*	
	Rural	*Urban*
Top 5 per cent	-	31.0
Top 10 per cent	33.6	42.4
Top 50 per cent	79.3	83.0
Bottom 20 per cent	4.0	4.0

Source: *NCAER, Urban Income and Saving (New Delhi, 1962), Quoted in the Report of the Committee (Mahalnobis Committee) on Distribution of Income and Levels of Living, p. 14.*

It is seen from Table 2.3 that top 10 percent of household sector garnered 42.4 per cent of aggregate income in urban sector as against 33.6 percent of rural income concerned by their counterpart in the rural sector. Top 50 per cent urban households enjoyed 83 per cent of urban income in contrast to 79.3 per cent of rural income by their counterparts in the rural sector. However, bottom 20 per cent households accounted for only 4 per cent of the respective incomes in rural and urban sectors. These observations clearly reveal that income inequality in the urban is more pronounced than in the rural areas.

It stems for the Table 2.4 that personal income distribution by decile groups or population is less skewed than by the decile groups of households; approximately 47.5 per cent of the disposable income has gone to top 20 per cent and about 7.5 per cent to the bottom 20 per cent of the population as against 49.2 per cent and 5.91 per cent to the top 20 per cent and bottom 20 per cent of the household respectively. The Lorenz ratio of 0.39 for the population is less than for the households estimated at 0.41. This table also shows that there is more unequal distribution of disposable income in urban sector with Lorenz ratio of 0.46 than the rural section having a Lorenz ratio of 0.35.

Table 2.4

Percentage Distribution of Disposable Personal Income by Decile Groups of Population and Households (NCAER, 1964-65)

Decile Groups of Population from Bottom (Percentage)	*% Share in Total Income*	*Rural Sector % Share in Total Income*	*Urban Sector % Share in Total Income*	*Total % Share in Total Income*
0-10	3.14	3.00	2.26	2.68
10-20	4.36	4.38	3.26	3.23
20-30	5.13	5.39	4.13	4.88
30-40	5.99	6.40	4.83	5.83
40-50	6.85	7.42	5.83	6.72
50-60	7.72	8.34	7.02	7.65
60-70	8.81	9.56	8.71	8.75
70-80	10.51	10.85	9.97	10.37
80-90	14.14	13.75	14.11	14.09
90-100	33.35	30.90	39.88	35.11
Bottom 20%	7.50	7.39	5.52	6.60
Top 20%	47.49	44.65	53.95	49.20
Lorenz Ratio	0.39	0.35	0.46	0.41

Source: The NCAER, All India Consumer Expenditure Survey, Vol. I & II, (New Delhi, 1966-67).

5. Estimates of Ojha and Bhatt

P.D. Ojha and V.V. Bhatt have in their joint study estimated the income distribution in India for two years; 1963-64 and 1964-65 by utilizing the CSO data on national income, estimates of direct taxes paid by unincorporated business and household saving data. Data derived from these sources have been used to estimate the aggregate consumption expenditure which is distributed among the decile expenditure groups of population on the basis of relevant NSS percentage distribution. Savings have been added to the consumption expenditure of the top most groups on the assumption that they are made only by the richest and this aggregate is taken as income (Y = C + S) of the group. For all other groups, income is taken equivalent to their consumption expenditure (Y = C). This methodology tends to under estimate the degree of inequality, for it ignores net dissaving of the lower expenditure groups. The main results of the study are tabulated below.

Table 2.5

Percentage Distribution of Disposable Personal Income

1963-64 & 1964-65

Decline Groups of Population from Bottom Percentage		*Average of 1663-64 & 1964-65*
0 – 10		3
10 – 20		4
20 – 30		5
30 – 40		6
40 – 50		6
50 – 60		7
60 – 70		9
70 – 80		12
80 – 90		13
90 – 100		36
Bottom	20%	7
Top	10%	48
Lorenz Ratio		0.375

Source: T.N. Srinivasan and P.K. Bardhan, *Poverty and Income Distribution in India,* Calcutta, 1974, p. 104.

The nature of income inequality is quite obvious from Table 2.5 as top 20 per cent of population accounts for 48 per cent of disposable personal income and the share of bottom 20 per cent of population is only 7 per cent. The high degree of inequality is also evident from the Lorenz ratio of 0.375.

6. Estimates of Ranadive

K.R. Ranadive in her estimates of income distribution for 1961-62 taxes care of the tax evasion by the rich and the net dissaving of the poor. She makes two alternative estimates on the basis of two sets of assumption.

i) the urban households with income less than Rs. 2,000 and rural households with income less than Rs. 720 have zero net savings and all evaded tax payments are fully reflected in consumption and/or savings.

ii) that urban households with income less than Rs. 3000 and rural households with income less than Rs. 1200 are assumed to have net dissavings. The net dissavings of the urban households in lower income bracket are assumed to be 25 per cent of the total urban savings, whereas for poor rural households are assumed to be 14 per cent of the total rural savings. The evasions are assumed not to be reflected in consumption and/or savings.

As a consequence, estimates based on second assumption show a greater degree of inequality than the estimates built around first assumption as 13 seen in Table 2.6.

Data in the Table 2.6 vividly reveals that income inequality under the second assumption with an estimated Lorenz ratio of 0.067 is higher than under the first assumption with the Lorenz ratio calculated at 0.351.

Table 2.6

Percentage Distribution of Disposable Personal Income

K.R. Ranadive (1961-62)

Decile Groups of Population from Bottom Percentage		*Ranadive 1961-62*	
		Assumption	*Assumption*
0 – 10		3.40	3.29
10 – 20		4.40	4.31
20 – 30		5.39	5.21
30 – 40		6.25	5.97
40 – 50		7.06	6.70
50 – 60		8.16	8.06
60 – 70		9.18	8.86
70 – 80		10.69	10.90
80 – 90		16.37	15.81
90 – 100		29.10	30.89
Bottom	20 %	7.80	7.60
Top	20 %	54.47	46.70
Lorenz Ratio		0.351	0.367

Source: T.N. Srinivasan and P.K. Bardhan, *Poverty and Income Distribution in India*, (Calcutta, 1974), p.104.

7. Madalgi's Estimates of Personal Income Distribution

S.S. Madalgi estimated personal income distribution for the year 1971 and arrived at the conclusion that personal income distribution is relatively more unequally distributed in the urban than in the rural areas. His findings are summarized in the Table 2.7.

It is evident from the Table 2.7 that the ratio of per capita income in the lowest to the highest expenditure class is higher (1:12.8) in urban than in the rural areas (1:8.7). Further, 8 per cent of the urban population in the expenditure class of Rs. 55 and above enjoys 40.1 per cent of disposable income as against 2.8 per cent of population enjoying 13.6 per cent disposable income in the rural areas. It is thus obvious that there is affluence of the few and poverty of the mass of population.

Table 2.7

Personal Income Distribution in India in 1971-72 At 1960-61 Prices

Monthly Expen-diture Class (in Rs.)	*Per Capita Annual Income (in Rs.)*		*Disposable Income as % of Total Income*		*Population in Expenditure as % of Total Population*	
	Rural	*Urban*	*Rural*	*Urban*	*Rural*	*Urban*
0 – 18	187	168	30.8	13.1	54.0	35.1
18 – 21	299	251	10.5	6.5	11.5	11.8
21 – 28	363	313	17.1	12.8	15.5	18.6
28 – 34	477	400	1.6	8.5	7.9	9.8
34 – 43	577	487	10.1	9.4	5.4	8.9
43 – 55	731	616	6.3	9.6	2.9	7.2
55 & above	1636	2149	13.6	40.1	2.8	8.6

Source: Complied from S.S. Madalgi, *Population and Food Survey in India,* p. 81.

Briefly, all these studies suggest that during the period under review, income inequalities in the country were quite pronounced, however, distribution of income in the rural areas was less skewed than in the urban areas. Tendulkar for this analysis of the pattern of income distribution divided the planned development period into two phases, viz., sustained growth phase or phase I covering a period of first Three Five Year Plans (1950-51 to 1964-65) and declaration phase or phase II covering a period from 1964-65 to 1973-74 and made the following observations:

"The Gini co-efficient for the rural population decreased where as that for the urban population increase during the sustained growth phase. The structure of the size distribution of person (pre-tax) household incomes at current prices did not change at the all-India level between 1953-54 to 1964-65. The declaration phase, since the mid-sixties is marked by a movement in the opposite direction. The Gini co-efficient for the rural sector recorded an increase and that for the urban sector decline between 1964-65 and 1975-76 with all-India co-efficient showing no signs of change".

Partial support to these observations have been lent by the findings of an all-India Household Survey conducted by NCAER in 1972, the results of which are presented in the Table 2.8.

Table 2.8

Percentage Share of Household Disposable Income in Aggregate Income for Different Fractile Groups

	Percentage Share in Disposable Income				
Fractile	*1962*		*1967-68*		*All India*
Group	*Urban*	*Rural*	*Urban*	*Rural*	
0 – 10	1.3	2.1	2.0	1.8	1.8
10 – 20	2.8	3.8	3.2	3.2	3.0
20 – 30	3.7	4.7	4.3	3.8	3.7
30 – 40	4.7	5.6	4.9	4.5	4.6
40 – 50	6.6	6.3	6.1	5.7	5.8
50 – 60	6.7	8.2	7.3	7.1	7.0
60 – 70	8.3	9.5	8.9	8.8	9.0
70 – 80	10.7	11.7	10.0	11.8	11.8
80 – 90	15.8	15.3	15.6	17.3	16.9
90 – 100	40.4	32.8	36.9	36.1	36.5
Lorenz Co-efficient of Concentration	0.49	0.41		0.46	0.46

Source: NCAER, *All India Household Survey of Income, Savings and Consumer Expenditure,* (December 1971), p. 26.

Analysis of Table 2.8 indicates that share of the bottom 20 per cent households in the disposable income has declined from 5.9 per cent in 1962 to 5.0 per cent in 1967-68 while as the share of top 20 per cent household recorded a rise from 48.1 per cent to 53.4 per cent during the same period. This suggests a tendency towards increasing concentration in the rural household sector. In the urban sector, bottom 20 per cent households accounted for 5.2 per cent of disposable income in 1967-68 as against 4.1 per cent in 1962 whereas the share of top 20 per cent of the households decreased from 56.2 per cent in 1962 to 52.5 per cent in 1967-68. This indicates a trend towards decline in the degree of inequality in the urban areas. The rise in the Lorenz Co-efficient of concentration for rural areas from 0.41 in 1962 to 0.46 in 1967-68 and decline for urban areas from 0.49 in 1962 to 0.46 in 1967-68 substantiate the above conclusion.

Trends in Consumer Expenditure

Study of the differentials in the levels of living is better concerned with the help of the analysis of size distribution of the consumer expenditure because the level of living tend to a fairly stable and their range of variation across different sections of the population is limited. Also because a fairly comparable series for the size distribution of per capita expenditure (at current prices) is available from the National Sample Survey Organisation Dandekar and Rath made a pioneering study of the NSS data on the consumer expenditure for the period 1960-61 and 1967-68, results of which are presented in the Table 2.9.

Information provided by this Table reveals that all sections of rural population recorded an increase in the per capita expenditure from 1960-61, to 1967-68, excepting the bottom 5 per cent in whose case it remained stable at Rs. 75. However, in the urban areas per capita expenditure of the bottom 50 per cent population showed a decline while as the top 50 per cent population experienced an increase during the same period. This indicates an improvement in the levels of living in the rural areas as against worsening of the situation for the bottom 50 per cent of the urban population. However, wide disparity in the per capita expenditure of the bottom and top sections of population in both the rural and urban areas is quite apparent suggesting that the gains of development have been appropriated by the richer classes and the living standards of the lower income groups have either remained stationery or have positively deteriorated.

Table 2.9

Per Capita Annual Consumer Expenditure in Different Sections of Rural and Urban Population in 1960-61 and 1967-68 (1960-61 Prices)

Section of Population	*Rural*		*Urban*	
	1960-61 (Rs.)	*1967-68 (Rs.)*	*1960-61 (Rs.)*	*1967-68 (Rs.)*
0 – 5	75	75	96	78
5 – 10	100	102	130	112
10 – 20	124	127	156	146
20 – 30	150	153	191	183
30 – 40	174	179	224	220
40 – 50	198	205	257	256
50 – 60	227	206	297	304
60 – 70	259	270	343	359
70 – 80	303	316	421	442
80 – 90	382	399	554	580
90 – 95	493	515	753	790
95 – 100	871	909	1269	1230
All Sections	259	209	356	364

Source: V.M. Dandekar and N. Rath, *Poverty in India.*

The Planning Commission arrives at an identical conclusion, Government of India from its estimates of distribution of consumption expenditure on the basis of 32nd Round of National Sample Survey as is evident from Table 2.10.

Table 2.10

Distribution of Total Private Consumption Expenditure by Deciles, 1977-78

Decline	*Rural (%)*	*Urban (%)*
0 – 10	3.7	3.4
10 – 20	5.1	4.7
20 – 30	6.2	5.6
30 – 40	6.6	6.5
40 – 50	8.0	7.4
50 – 60	8.7	8.7
60 – 70	9.8	9.8
70 – 80	11.8	12.3
80 – 90	14.5	14.2
90 – 100	25.6	27.4
0 – 100	100.00	120.0

Source: The Sixth Plan (1980-85).

It is observed from the Table 2.10 that in the rural areas bottom 20 per cent of the population accounts for 8.8 per cent of total private consumption expenditure as against 40.1 per cent enjoyed by the top 20 per cent of the population. In the urban areas, share of the bottom 20 per cent population in the total private consumption expenditure is estimated at 8.1 per cent while as the share of top 20 per cent population is calculated at 41.6 per cent. These observations suggested their private consumption expenditure is highly unevenly distributed in the both the rural as well as the urban areas.

It is observed from the Table 2.10 that in the rural areas bottom 20 per cent of the population accounts for 8.8 per cent of total private consumption expenditure as against 40.1 per cent enjoyed by the top 20 per cent of the population. In the urban areas, share of the bottom 20 per cent population in the total private consumption expenditure is estimated at 8.1 per cent while as the share of top 20 per cent population

Table 2.11

Gini Co-efficient of the Size Distribution of Normal Per Capita Household Private Consumption Expenditure

Sl. No.	*Year*	*Rural*	*India*	*Urban*	*India*
1.	1953-54	0.334		0.381	
2.	1954-55	3.350		0.390	
3.	1955-56	0.344		0.368	
4.	1956-57	0.332		0.394	
5.	1957-58	0.344		0.359	
6.	1958-59	0.340		0.348	
7.	1959-60	0.314		0.357	
8.	1960-61	0.321	0.321	0.350	0.348
9.	1961-62	0.312	0.313	0.357	0.357
10.	1962-63	NA	NA	NA	NA
11.	1963-64	0.297	0.297	0.360	0.360
12.	1964-65	0.294	0.294	0.360	0.349
13.	1965-66	NA	0.297	NA	0.339
14.	1966-67	NA	0.293	NA	0.337
15.	1967-68	0.293	0.291	0.345	0.332
16.	1968-69		0.305		0.329
17.	1969-70		0.293		0.340
18.	1970-71		0.283		0.327
19.	1971-72	NA	NA	NA	NA
20.	1972-73		0.299		0.341
21.	1973-74		0.276		
22.	1974-75				
23.	1975-76				
24.	1976-77				
25.	1977-78		0.336		0.344
26.	1983		0.297		0.325

Source: Columns (2) and (4) from GS. Chatterjee and N. Bhattacharya, "On Disparities in Per Capita Household Consumption in India". In T. N. Srinivasan and P.K. Bardhan (eds.), *Poverty and Income Distribution in India*, Statistical Publishing Society, Calcutta, 1974. Columns (3) and (5) from S.P. Gupta and K.L. Datta, "Poverty Calculations in the Sixth Plan", *Economic and Political Weekly*, April 14, 1984.

is calculated at 41.6 per cent. These observations suggested their private consumption expenditure is highly unevenly distributed in both the rural as well as the urban areas.

Tendulkar has compiled from different sources, the Gini Co-efficient calculated on the basis of NSS data and the same are presented in Table 2.11.

It appears from the Table 2.11 that the Gini Co-efficient for the rural population declined slightly from 0.33 in 1953-54 to 0.32 in 1960-61 and further to 0.293 in 1967-68, Gini Co-efficient for the urban population is also seen to have declined from 0.39 in themed 1950's to 0.35 by 1960-61, followed by a rise to 0.36 in 1963-64 and a decline to 0.345 in 1967-68.

Tendulkar poses a question as to whatever the observed reduction in the inequality is a purely monetary illusion (because of changing prices over time) or whether it could be taken to hold in real terms as well. He attempted an answer on the basis of the relative price movements for different decile groups of population and concluded that the greater reduction in the urban Gini Co-efficient than the rural one from 1953-54 to 1960-61 may be expected to hold in real terms. However, during the four years (1960-61 to 1964-65 the reduction observed for the rural population would overstate the reduction in real terms. Whereas for the urban population, there may have been a worsening of relative inequality because of the continuation of the regressive price rise during the later years may be expected to result in the decline in Gini Co-efficient over-stating the reduction in the relative inequality in real terms for the urban population. A slight reduction recorded in nominal terms for the rural population could possibly reflect worsening or unchanged relative inequality in real terms when compared to 1954-65. Foregoing discussion inevitably suggests that the relative inequality in levels of living in real terms has been lower towards the mid – 1970's than in the early 1950's. It is further seen that the Gini-co-efficient rose in 1977-78 and fell again in 1983.

Iyengar and Brahamnanda estimates the Gini-Lorenz Ratio on the basis of the various rounds of NSS data to analyse the movements in the consumer expenditure pattern in rural and urban areas. Their estimates of Gini-Lorenz Ratio are presented in Table 2.12 & 2.13.

Table 2.12

Lorenz Ratio

Year	*Round*	*Rural*	*Urban*
1952	4th	0.340	0.365
1953-53	5th	0.330	0.397
1953-54	7th	0.334	0.371
1954-55	8th	0.350	0.370
1955	9th	0.335	0.371
1955-56	10th	0.344	0.368
1956-57	11th	0.319	0.402
1957	12th	0.331	0.393
1957-58	13th	0.333	0.377
1958-59	14th	0.328	0.348
1959-60	15th	0.314	0.357
1960-61	16th	0.321	0.350
1961-62	17th	0.316	0.362
1962-64	18th	0.300	0.366
1964-65	19th	0.297	0.357
1965-66	20th	0.301	0.347
1966-67	21st	0.298	0.349
1967-68	22nd	0.296	0.348
1968-69	23rd	0.310	0.346
1969-70	24th	2.298	0.362
1970-71	26th	0.289	0.352
1972-73	27th	0.304	0.348
1973-74	28th	0.282	0.310
1977-78	32nd	0.340	0.352
1983	38th	0.296	0.332

Source: NSS Data.

Table 2.13

Plan-wise Average Gini-Lorenz Ratio

Plan		*Number of Observations*	*Rural*	*Urban*
I	(1951-1956)	6	0.34	0.38
II	(1956-1960)	6	0.33	0.37
III	(1961-1965)	4	0.30	0.35
	(1961-1968)	3	0.30	0.33
IV	(1969-1973)	4	0.29	0.33
V	(1974-1979)	1	0.31	0.33
	(1979-1980)	NA	NA	NA
VI	(1980-1984)	1	0.30	0.33

* *Annual Plans.*

Analysis of the information contained in Table 2.12 and 2.13 reveals that inequality in the consumer expenditure pattern was higher during the 1950's than in the subsequent decades, for observed Gini-Lorenz Ratio is consistently declining in both the rural as well as the urban areas from 0.34 and 0.38 respectively during 1951-56 to 0.29 to 0.33 during 1969-73. However, the Gini-Lorenz Ratio for the rural areas rose to 0.31 during 1974-79 but fell again to 0.30 during all these years. It is also obvious that the distribution in the rural areas has tended to become stable from the early sixties while as far urban areas stability is observed from the late sixties onwards. Another noticeable observation is that the Gini-Lorenz Ratio for the urban areas is higher than the rural areas during the entire period, suggesting that inequality is more pronounced in the former than in the latter areas. These conclusions are further supported by the analysis of the relative percentage shares of the bottom half of the population (Q 0.5) in the consumption expenditure for the period 1952 and 1983 as contained in the Table 2.14.

Table 2.14

The Relative Percentage Share of Bottom Half of Population (Q 0.5) in Consumption Expenditure

Year	*Share of Bottom Half*	
	Rural	*Urban*
1952	27.41	25.23
1952-53	27.75	23.55
1953-54	27.53	24.91
1954-55	25.98	24.04
1955-56	26.84	25.14
1957	28.12	25.02
1957-58	27.81	26.04
1959-60	29.94	26.82
1960-61	28.40	26.39
1961-62	29.07	25.87
1963-64	30.14	26.18
1964-65	30.38	26.71
1965-66	30.00	27.30
1966-67	30.90	27.40
1967-68	30.20	27.40
1968-69	29.50	27.60
1969-70	30.30	27.00
1970-71	30.90	27.40
1972-73	30.40	27.60
1973-74	31.40	29.80
1977-78	29.60	27.50
1983	30.00	28.10

Source: NSS Rounds.

Perusal of the information given in the Table 2.14 reveals that the relative percentage share of the bottom half of population in consumption expenditure is higher in rural than in the urban areas for the entire period from 1952 to 1983, thus showing lesser degree of inequality in rural than in urban areas. The data also shows an improvement in the levels of living in both rural as well as urban areas, for relative shares in these areas have moved upward.

Table 2.15

Estimates of Per Capita Consumption and Lorenz Ratio Based on Current Price Distribution – India (Rural and Urban), 1961-62 to 1973-74

Year	*Per Capita Consumption (Rs. Per Month)*		*Lorenz Ratio*	
	Rural	*Urban*	*Rural*	*Urban*
1961-62	21.73	30.86	0.3130	0.3566
1963-64	22.37	32.96	0.2974	0.3596
1964-65	26.44	36.03	0.2936	0.3492
1965-66	30.90	41.54	0.2934	0.3368
1967-68	33.40	44.82	0.2908	0.3324
1968-69	33.29	46.04	0.3051	0.3292
1969-70	34.70	50.34	0.2928	0.3403
1970-71	35.31	52.85	0.2831	0.3265
1972-73	44.17	63.33	0.2993	0.3410
1973-74	53.01	70.77	0.2758	0.3013

Source: Suryanarayan, (1980).

Some other studies such as those of Iyengar and Bhattacharya and Vaidyanathan pointed out that price unadjusted consumption distribution do not reveal the underlying trends in real consumption distribution since price movements have differential impacts on different segments of the distribution. Iyengar and Jain observed that the decile-wise price movements are of the type that the poorer sections were affected by inflation more severely than the rich during the period 1963-64 to 1973-74. Radhakrishna and Sharma estimated that the inequalities in the living levels, after adjustment for prices started widening during the period beginning from 1963-64. Iyengar and Suryanarayana estimated the per capita consumption and

Lorenz Ratio's based on current price distributions separately for the rural and urban sectors of India for the period 1961-62 to 1973-74. The findings of the study are summed up in Table 2.15.

Perusal of the data given in Table 2.15 shows a perceptible increase in the per capita consumption expenditure and also an improvement in the distribution as is indicated by a decline in the Lorenz Ratio's for both the rural and urban sectors during the period under study. This may suggest a marked increase in aggregate welfare in the rural and urban sectors of India. However, estimates made by them on the basis of deflated distribution show that the movements in the real magnitudes are different from those revealed by the price unadjusted estimates as is seen from Table 2.16.

Table 2.16

Estimate of Per Capita Consumption and Lorenz Ratio (at 1961-62 Prices) – India (Rural and Urban), 1961-62 to 1973-74

Year	*Per Capita Consumption (Rs. Per Month)*		*Lorenz Ratio*	
	Rural	*Urban*	*Rural*	*Urban*
1961-62	21.73	30.86	0.3100	0.3560
1963-64	20.31	30.24	0.3000	0.3630
1964-65	20.88	29.51	0.3080	0.3640
1965-66	20.84	27.90	0.3090	0.3540
1966-67	19.78	27.94	0.3120	0.3620
1967-68	18.80	27.19	0.3150	0.3650
1968-69	19.49	28.58	0.3260	0.3550
1969-70	19.45	29.75	0.3140	0.3640
1970-71	19.30	30.14	0.3010	0.3490
1972-73	20.58	32.96	0.3220	0.3710
1973-74	21.51	30.60	0.2990	0.3460

Source: Suryanarayan, (1980).

It is observed from Table 2.16 that the per capita consumption did not indicate any significant trend is either of the two sectors. It fell in the early part of the period and rose more or less steadily from around 1967-68 onwards, in both the sectors. The Lorenz Ratio's also did not show any consistent trend. They fluctuated around a stagnant trend in both rural and urban sectors. On the basis of these findings they concluded that consumption and inequality levels remained stagnant in the two sectors during 1961-62 to 1973-74.

On the basis of foregoing discussion, following broad conclusions are arrived at:

i) Inequality is more pronounced in the pattern of income distribution than in the distribution of consumer expenditure.

ii) Degree of inequality in income as well as expenditure is higher in urban than in the rural areas of India.

iii) In equality in the distribution of income and expenditure in both the rural and urban sectors has declined at current prices while, as at constant prices no firm trend is evident.

Incidence of Absolute Poverty

Generally, measurement of the prevalence of poverty is attempted with the help of two approaches viz., direct approach and income approach. According to the 'direct' approach, minimum levels of one or a combination of essential basis needs are specified and the incidence of poverty is measured in terms of the proportion of the population that falls below these levels. In the 'income' approach poverty is measured in terms of the proportion of the population with less than the minimum income needed to acquire some basic bundles of goods and services. This is not to say that the two are not linked. On the basis of these two approaches, experts including the Planning Commission to evaluate the extent and dimensions of poverty in India have made numerous studies from time to time. In most of the studies, incidence of poverty has been measured in terms of the percentage of the total population below a normatively specified poverty line reflecting basically some 'low enough' yet 'reasonable' minimum level of living besides controversies centering around the elements of subjectivity in the 'low enough' and 'reasonable' concepts, data deficiencies and unresolved methodological issues have made it extremely difficult to obtain a comprehensive picture of poverty in India. Despite these lacunae, estimates relating to the incidence of poverty made by various experts including Planning Commission are helpful in understanding the nature and extent of poverty in the country. Accordingly main points of some of the studies made on the incidence of poverty in India are summarized in the subsequent pages to comprehend magnitude of the problem.

In 1962, Government of India appointed a study group comprising Prof. D.R. Gadgil, B.N. Ganguly, P.S. Lokanathan, M.R. Masani, Ashok Mehta, Shriman Narayan, Pitamber Pant, V.K.R.V. Rao and Anna Sahib Saharasbudhe that recommended a standard private consumption of Rs. 20 per capita per month as demarcating the poverty line. The group excluded expenses on medical and educational facilities from the total computed expenditure on the assumption that these shall be distributed cost-free by the state in accordance with its constitutional obligations. These recommendations of the group are criticized on the basis that 'a per capita per month' expenditure of Rs. 20 without a reference to the prices of a number of essential commodities does not make clear the implied level of living sufficiently explicit. Further, it does not make any distinction between rural and urban living costs.

P.O. Ojha (1970) in one of his studies estimates both rural and urban poverty for 1960-61 and rural poverty for 1967-68 by using diet intake of 2,250 calories per capita per day and NSS data on personal expenditure. He assumes that 66 per cent of this calorie intake must be obtained from grains, cereals and pulses in urban areas while as the corresponding figure for rural areas was 80 per cent. On the basis of these assumptions he works out the food requirement at 518 g and 432 g per day person in rural and urban areas respectively. By adopting NSS data, he reaches the conclusion that in rural areas (1960-61) for per capita expenditure range from 0.00 to Rs. 15-18, there existed deficiencies in food grain consumption in relation to minimum calorie requirements. For the urban population, nutritional deficiency persisted for individuals in two expenditure groups i.e., from Rs. 0-8 and Rs. 8-11 per month. From these findings, he concludes that the demarcation line between the poor and non-poor should be Rs. 18 per month in the rural areas and Rs. 11 in the urban areas. On this basis, he estimates that in 1960-61, approximately 51.8% of the rural population as 184.2 million people and 7.6 per cent or 6 million people in urban areas lived in poverty. He also concluded that in 1967-68, 70 per cent of the rural population was below the minimum level of foodgrains consumption.

Ojha's study suffers from certain drawbacks. It has not included the expenditure on health, education and housing while estimating the poverty line. The study has adopted the uniform minimum nutritional requirements i.e., 2,250 calories per person per day for the rural and urban population despite differences in socio-economic and cultural environment which in turn cause the difference in the calorie intake requirements in these settings. Further, price differentials in the two areas have also been ignored while calculating the poverty line.

Following the recommendation of the study group, B.S. Minhas (1970) adopts the figure of Rs. 240 per person per annum as a poverty line for the urban areas, however, for rural population a low figure of Rs. 200 is considered appropriate by him on the ground that rural cost of living trends to be lower at 1960-61 prices. On the basis of both the figures, he estimates the extent of poverty in the rural areas, the findings are summarized in the Table 2.17.

Table 2.17

Percentage and Number of People Below Minimum Levels of Living

	Below Rs. 240 Per Annum		*Below Rs. 200 Per Annum*	
Year	*% age*	*Million*	*% age*	*Million*
1956-57	65.0	215	52.4	173
1957-58	63.2	212	50.4	169
1960-61	59.4	211	46.0	164
1961-62	56.4	206	43.6	159
1963-64	57.8	221	44.2	169
1964-65	51.6	200	39.2	154
1967-68	50.6	210	37.1	154

Source: B.S. Minhas, (1970).

It is observed from Table 2.17 that the number of people below the poverty line of Rs. 200 decreased from 193 million in 1956-57 to 154 million in 1967-68 i.e., from 52.6 per cent of rural population to 37.1 per cent in the respective years. It is also seen that number of people below the poverty line of Rs. 240 decreased marginally from 215 million to 210 million while as the percentage decline from 65.0 to 50.6 was significant. This decline is largely explained by the growth in the average per capita consumption in real rather than by the slight fall in the concentration index of consumer expenditure. He further concludes that the number of poor tend to rise in bad harvest years.

Bardhan (1970) questions the validity of the GNP deflator as used by Minhas on the ground that is covers both agricultural and manufactured commodities and as such has a tendency to understate the rise in price paid by the rural poor because his budget includes a much smaller proportion of the manufacturers than the national average. Instead, he adopts the official agricultural labour consumer price index for deflating the consumption of the rural poor and the working class consumer price index for deflating the consumption of the urban poor. Like many other researchers, he relies on the NSS data on consumption expenditure. Thus, he draws the poverty line for rural sector at Rs. 15 and for urban sector at Rs. 18 at 1960-61 prices on the ground that the rural prices are generally lower than the urban prices. Accordingly, he estimates 135 million persons constituting 38 per cent of rural population as rural poor and 34 million people comprising 44 per cent of the urban population as urban poor in 1960-61. Using the same norms both for rural and urban areas, he suggests that at 1960-61 prices in 1968-69 as many as 54 per cent of the rural population and 41 per cent of the urban population were poor.

One of the major objections against the methodology adopted by Bardhan particularly regarding the uses of agricultural labour consumer price index for deflating the consumption of the rural poor is that small farmers is very large numbers are also included in the category of rural poor and their consumption pattern is not necessarily the same as that of agricultural labourers. Secondly, the appropriateness of the price imputed for consumption of self-produced agricultural commodities is also questionable. Lastly, Bardhan uses Rs. 15 as poverty line by excluding the expenditure on vegetables, nuts, education, health etc. from the food basket of the Pay Commission Report, while as, before using the NSS based average retail prices, he marks them down to take account of the fact that the average rural consumer does not procure all of his consumption needs from the market, a part of his supply being from his own home grown stock.

E.P.W. De Costa (1971) with the help of NSS data on the consumer expenditure for the year 1963-64, estimated poverty in three rings: (1) Severe destitution (2) Destination and (3) Poverty. The types of "poverty line" on the basis of monthly per capita expenditure, as indicated in Table 2.18, define the three rings of poverty level.

Table 2.18

Scale of Poverty Line E.P.W. De Costa

S. No.	*Years*	*Sever Destitute*		*Destitute*		*Poor*	
		Rural	*Urban*	*Rural*	*Urban*	*Rural*	*Urban*
1.	1960-61	11	15	13	18	15	21
2.	1964-65	15	21	18	24	21	28
3.	1970-71	21	28	28	34	28	43
4.	1973-74	28	34	34	42	43	55

Source: Mishra, Anand Prasad, *Rural Poverty in India,* Deep and Deep Publications, New Delhi, 1988, p. 162.

On the basis of three rings of poverty, population falling under the categories of severe destination, destitution and poverty was estimated by De Costa at 61.7 million, 104.4 million and 161.6 million corresponding to 13.2 per cent, 22.4 per cent and 34.4 per cent respectively in 1960-61.

Dandekar and Rath (1971) in their widely discussed and debated study assumed that the lowest minimum physical requirement of the diet is around 2,250 calories as against FAO estimates of 1,486 calories. With the help of the NSS data, they calculated that for rural areas in 1960-61, an annual per capita consumer expenditure of Rs. 170.8 was required to ensure a diet equivalent to 2,250 calories per capita per day while as in urban areas an amount of Rs. 270.7 was needed to purchase the same amount of nutrition. Thus, according to them, the urban consumer would have needed to spend roughly 59 per cent more to attain the same level of nutrition, whereas the average urban income was only 37 per cent higher. After rounding off the consumer expenditure estimates, they calculated that Rs. 15 per capita per month in the rural areas and Rs. 22.5 in the urban areas are required to purchase the food basket consistent with calories requirement of 2,250. Accordingly, they estimated that in 1960-61, about 33.12 per cent of the rural population and about 48.64 per cent of the urban population lived below the level of poverty. In their attempt to examine as to how the gains of development have been shared between different sections of population during the 1960's, they noted that the average consumer expenditure rose by only 4.8 per cent in the rural terms in the eight-year period. They also conclude that the process of development has benefited the upper middle and the richer sections much more than the middle, lower middle and the poor sections. Under the circumstances a certain amount of inequality is inevitable. As regards the urban population, "the lower middle and poorer sections constituting the bottom 40 per cent of the urban population have not benefited at all by the economic development. Indeed, the evidence is that their per capita consumption has declined and greatly so among the poorest 10 per cent". Thus, they conclude that urban poverty had deepened during 1960-61 and 1968-69, although average urban income still exceeded the average rural income, albeit by a small margin. They considered a per capita annual expenditure of Rs. 324 in the rural areas and Rs. 486 in the urban areas (at 1968-69 prices) as necessary for minimum level of living. On the basis of 50 per cent of urban population – in all 223.5 million people out of 532.7 million – are found to be living below the minimum level.

Madalgi stated that Dandekar and Rath have not given any scientific explanation for adopting 490 g as the nutritionally required quantity of food grains for the urban people and 616 g for rural people. He argued that if the food grains consumption level of NSS were reliable aggregate annual consumption of food-grains derived from per capita per month figures of NSS should have been somewhere near the figure of national availability derived from production imports etc. That is not so Desai stated that Dandekar and Rath are wrong in taking the average requirement. They are equally wrong in not taking into account the different requirements of different age groups, sex and so on and in basing their calculations on all-India average of calorie intake. Further by ignoring the type, nature and intensity of activities carried on in the rural and urban areas, they have either underestimated the people falling below the poverty line in the rural areas or over-estimated the urban poor. The NSS consumer expenditure estimates for 1967-68 and 1968-69 are based on quick tabulations of unscrutinised data and have been considered incredible even by Dandekar and Rath, for couple of reasons. First, it was noted that NSS estimates of rural per capita consumption in 1967-68 (deflated by national income deflator with 1960-61 base) was about 7 per cent below the corresponding NSS estimates in 1960-61 and about 11 per cent below the corresponding estimates in 1967-68 derived from official national accounts data. Secondly, they found that the average per capita consumption of the lowest 5 per cent rural Fractile group in 1967-68 was 94 per cent of that in 1960-61, while as for top 3 per cent Fractile group, the 1967-68 estimate was only 73 per cent of that in 1960-61. Such a large differential fall in the per capita consumption of the richest 3 per cent was against their a-priori-judgement. Hence, they revised the NSS estimates of per capita consumption in different sections of the rural population to firm with the official estimates of average rural consumption. It is, however, difficult to accept the authenticity of either of these two estimates without further investigation. Lastly, as stated by Shastry, the use of national income deflator to convert the current price data with 1960-61 prices is open to objection because deflating consumption by 'a deflator', which includes both consumption and investment goods, is illogical. During 1960's, the prices of agricultural commodities rose at a much sharper rate than those of finished manufactures. But since, the weight of the manufactured consumables in the budget of the rural poor is likely to be much lower than the national average (which includes the rich and poor, the urban as well as the rural sector), the national income deflator is very much likely to have under-stated the rise in the prices paid by the rural poor. Even within the class of agricultural commodities particularly cereals, there is evidence that the average price paid by the poor rose at a faster rate than by the rich. Further, since the weight of services in the budget of the rural poor is likely to be low, the national income deflator, which includes the price to be low, the national income deflator, which includes the price of services (whose index has grown at a relatively small rate), is likely to under-state the general price rise for the rural poor.

Vaidyanathan by taking an income level of Rs. 132 per annum to denote poverty, finds that 15.7 per cent of the rural population in 1960-61 was living in poverty. He also observes that the NSS data and the national income statistics yield different estimates of the degree of poverty as can be seen from Table 2.19.

Perusal of the Table reveals that as per NSS data, the degree of poverty has increased while as according to official series a marginal decline is recorded from 1960-61 to 1967-68.

Table 2.19

Poverty Estimates Rural Areas

(In Million People)

Year	*N.S.S.*	*Official Series*
1960-61	59.5	58.0
1964-65	60.4	46.9
1967-68	67.8	57.8

Source: A. Vaidyanathan, (1974).

Bhatty adopts Sen's measure of poverty, Ps. and head count ratio to estimate the incidence of poverty among the various occupational groups in rural areas. Results of his study are summarized in Table 2.20.

It is observed from the Table 2.20 that for all poverty levels above Rs. 180 per capita per annum, the incidence of poverty was most severe among agricultural labourers and least among cultivators. Since the data pertain only to one year i.e., 1968-69, therefore it is not possible to show whether poverty has been increasing or not.

Table 2.20

Proportions of Rural People Below the Poverty Line (1968-69)

Categories	*Rs. 15/-*	*Rs. 20/-*	*Rs. 25/-*	*Rs. 30/-*	*Rs. 35/-*
Cultivators (% age)	22.66	38.31	52.48	62.36	70.28
Agricultural Labourers (% age)	31.64	56.21	71.36	82.84	89.56
Non-Agricultural Workers (% age)	21.95	39.55	55.87	69.70	79.77
All Households (% age)	24.19	42.43	56.41	67.15	75.02

Source: Bhatty, (1974), Tables 11-14, pp. 318-19.

Sukhatme observed that nutritional requirement of 2100-2400 calories as adopted by most of the studies to estimates incidence of poverty in India is not the minimum but recommended average. He points out that in a population which is normally distributed with respect to height, weight, activity rate etc., half of the people will have a calorie requirement below this recommended average. By comparison of the distribution of requirements with the distribution of intake, the actual number of under-nourished persons would be smaller. According to this norm he estimates the population below the poverty line at 25 per cent and 15 per cent of the urban and rural areas.

Food and Agricultural Organisation estimate of poverty is based on Basal Metabolic Rate (BMR), the critical energy input required to maintain human body. The F.A.O. set a minimum limit of 1.2 BMR i.e., 1,486 calories below which, is a situation of energy deprivation. The proportion of people below this critical level was estimated at about 30 per cent of total population in 1972-73.

Table 2.21

Incidence of Poverty in Rural India Estimates of Ahluwalia

Period	*No. of Poor (Millions)*	*% Age of Rural Population Below the Poverty Line*
1960-61	152.0	42.0
1961-62	157.0	42.3
1963-64	189.0	49.1
1964-65	198.0	50.4
1965-66	206.0	51.1
1966-67	235.0	57.1
1967-68	245.0	57.9
1968-69	227.0	53.5
1970-71	217.0	49.1
1973-74	221.0	47.6

Source: Ahluwalia, Montek S., "Rural Poverty and Agricultural Performance in India". *The Journal of Development Studies*, April, 1978, pp. 289-292.

Ahluwalia, estimates the degree of poverty in rural India for eighteen years period from 1956-57 to 1973-74 and adopts consumer expenditure of Rs. 15 per capita per month at 1960-61 rural prices as the poverty line. He calculates equivalent poverty lines for the period under study with the help of consumer price indices for agricultural labourers. He also used the head count ratio and Sen's poverty index Ps. to calculate the incidence of poverty. Findings of his study are presented in Table 2.21.

Analysis of Table 2.21 clearly shows that the incidence of poverty during 1960's recorded a substantial increase to as much as 241 million people constituting 57.9 per cent of the rural population in 1967-68. However, thereafter, a steady decline in the degree of poverty is seen. Ahluwalia also observed a significant inverse relationship between the performance of agricultural sector and rural poverty.

The Seventh Finance Commission reflected the earliest estimates of the poverty line as being too narrow. The commission developed a concept of an augmented poverty line according to which monthly private consumption expenditure is augmented by the per capita monthly public expenditure by each state government under various heads such as education, social welfare, roads, water supply and sanitation, health and family planning and administration of courts, jails and police. According to thus augmented poverty line, the commission concludes that in 1970-71, 53 per cent of rural and 51 per cent of the urban population lived below the poverty line.

One of the avowed objectives of economic planning in India is to alleviate the poverty of its teeming millions. With the view to comprehend the nature and magnitude of poverty, the Planning Commission constituted a working group in 1962, which suggested that those with a per capita monthly expenditure of Rs. 20 (at 1960-61 prices) be defined as poor. But this method was not incorporated in the Fourth and Fifth Plans, which only envisaged improving the consumption level of the bottom 30 per cent people. Only the Sixth Plan, was the parameter of poverty clearly defined and methodology spelt out in the technical note of the plan documented. Sixth Plan adopted the physical survival definition of poverty and identified poverty line as the mid-point of a monthly per capital expenditure of a class having a daily calories intake of 2,435 per person in rural areas and 2,095 calories per person in urban areas which worked out to Rs. 76 in rural areas and Rs. 88 in urban areas at 1979-80 prices. Those spending less than these sums were declared as poor. On this criterion the Planning Commission found that in 1979-80, 317 million persons constituting 48.4 per cent of the country's total population are living below the poverty line. Out of the total population of the poor, 260 million are residing in the rural areas and 57 million in the urban areas. In relative terms, 50.7 per cent of the rural population and 40.3 per cent of the urban population are categories as poor. In 1984-85 poor population is estimated at 272.7 million or 36.9 per cent of the total population, out of which 222.2 million or 39.9 per cent are living in the rural areas and 50.5 million constituting 27.7 per cent are residing in the urban areas. In the Seventh Five Year Plan, poverty line is estimated around Rs. 6,400 per annum of household income or approximately Rs. 107 per capita per month at 1984-85 prices. On this criterion, the Seventh Plan envisages the percentage of population with consumption standard below the poverty line to come down to 25.8 per cent by 1989-90. In absolute terms, the number of poor persons is expected to fall from 273 million in 1984-85 to 211 million in 1989-90. For the rural and urban areas, the respective figures are 168.6 million (28.2 per cent) and 42.2 million (19.3 per cent). Plan projections also suggest that the percentage of people below poverty line is expected to decline to 10 per by 1994-95 and further to a level of 5 per cent in the year 2000.

Authenticity of these estimates of the Planning Commission regarding the incidence of poverty has come under scathing criticism. Controversy centres on the number of persons estimated at 57 million by the Planning Commission to have crossed the poverty line because of the rise in their real incomes during 1980-81 and 1981-82. According to Raj Krishna after taking into account the impact of IRDP and NREP as well as the growth of GNP "the maximum number of poverty line crossers in the first two years of the Sixth Plan could only be 7.7 million and not 57 million". Therefore, his estimate of population in poverty is around 331 million *i.e.*, 48.8 per cent of total population (Raj, 1976). Vasant Gumaste observed that since under IRDP and NREP transfer of technology, assets and service (TAS) has tended to benefit the top layers of income category therefore, the likely number of families who have crossed over the poverty line should be about 1.4 million or 7 million persons

(Vasant, 1983). Sundaram and Tendulkar conclude that 11 million people plausibly have been pushed up above the poverty line by 1981-82. However, keeping in view, the results of 1981 census and the extent of under-estimation, "the incidence of poverty in 1981-82 would be 46.50 per cent of 329 million poor instead of 41.5 per cent or 282 million poor as estimated by the Planning Commission". It may be pointed out that the incidence of poverty over the years has been moving up and down following the trend of food grain production. The Planning Commission has also admitted this fact. The poverty level has been high in years when the agricultural production particularly food grains have been high. Since food grain constitute a major part of the consumption expenditure, the levels of the living, of poor move up in good agricultural years and move down during hard harvest. It is thus seen that in 1972-73 when food grain output was lower at 97 million tones as against 105 million tones in 1971-72, the poverty line jumped upto 51.5 per cent. In 1977-78, when the food grain production had gone up to 126.4 million tones from 121 million tones in 1976-77, the poverty level came down to 48.3 per cent. Again in 1983-84, when total production increased to 152.4 million tones as against 129.5 million tones in 1982-83, the poverty line came down to 42.6 per cent. If this trend were followed, it would mean that in 1984-85, when the food grain production decreased to 146 million tones, the poverty line would have jumped up and not falling down to 36.9 as estimated by the Planning Commission. Further, in view of the overall performances of the Indian economy during the last four decades, it is reasonable to conclude that the expectation of the Planning Commission to bring down percentage of population below the poverty line to 5 per cent is more a wishful thinking.

Precisely, the findings of the various studies regarding the incidence of poverty in rural India are summarized in Table 2.22.

Table 2.22

A Comparative Statement showing Different Estimates of Rural Poverty in India

Sr. No.	*Year*	*Organisation / Researcher*	*Estimated Number*	*% of Rural Population Below Poverty*	*Definition of Poverty Based on*
1	2	3	4	5	6
1.	1960-61	Dandekar & Rath	135.0	40.0	Rs. 1.80 per cent at 1960-61 prices yielding a minimum of 2,250 calories per day.
2.		Ahluwalia	152.0	42.0	Rs. 189 p.c., c.e., p.a., at 1960-61 prices.
		Vaidyanathan	213.3	59.5	Rs. 240 p.c., c.e., p.a., at 1960-61 prices.
		Ojha	184.2	51.8	Rs. 216 p.c., c.e., p.a., at 1960-61 prices.
3.	1961-62	Ahluwalia	157.0	42.3	Rs. 180 p.c., c.e., p.a., at 1960-61 prices.
4.	1962-63	NIRD	166.0	44.9	The regression equation between NDP from agriculture and Ahluwalia's time series estimates of incidence of poverty.

(Contd.)

1	2	3	4	5	6
5.	1963-64	E.P.W. De Costa	161.0	34.6	Three types of classification, destitutes, Severe destitutes and poor based on a minimum per capita expenditure per annum.
		D.S. Minhas	221.0	57.8	Two alternative levels of Rs. 240 and 200 per capita annual consumption expenditure at 1960-61 prices.
		Ahluwalia	189.0	49.1	Above mentioned criterion.
6.	1964-65	Vaidyanathan	235.7	60.0	As mentioned above Rs. 240 p.c., p.a., c.e.
		Bardhan	17.4	51.6	Rs. 180 p.c., c.e., p.a., at 1960-61,
		Ahluwalia	198.0	50.4	Above mentioned criterion.
7.	1965-66	Ahluwalia	205.0	51.1	Above mentioned criterion.
8.	1966-67	Ahluwalia	235.0	57.4	Above mentioned criterion.
9.	1967-68	Ahluwalia	241.0	27.9	Above mentioned criterion.
		Dandekar & Rath Vaidyanathan	166.4 -	40.0 67.8	Above mentioned criterion.

(Contd.)

1	2	3	4	5	6
					Above mentioned criterion.
		Minhas	210.0	50.6	Rs. 240 p.c., c.e., p.a.
		Ojha	289.0	70.0	Estimates of minimum desirable income *i.e.*, Rs. 216 to Rs. 480 per annum.
10.	1968-69	Ahluwalia	227.0	53.5	Above mentioned criterion.
11.	1969-70	AFICCI	218.3	41.2	Rs. 240, p.c., c.e., p.a., at 1960-61 prices.
		NIRD	196.0	42.2	Earlier mentioned criterion.
12.	1970-71	Ahluwalia	217.0	49.1	Earlier mentioned criterion.
		IIPC	198.9	45.0	Rs. 336 p.c., c.e., p.a.
13.	1971-72	NIRD	183.0	41.5	Earlier mentioned criterion.
14.	1972-73	NIRD	212.0	47.2	Earlier mentioned criterion.
		Planning Commission	200.0	35.6	Rs. 480 p.c., c.e., p.a., at 1972-73 prices.
15.	1973-74	Ahluwalia	221.0	47.6	Earlier mentioned criterion.
		IIPO	208.0	44.8	Rs. 516 p.c., c.e., p.a.

(Contd.)

1	2	3	4	5	6
16.	1974-75	NIRD	232.0	50.1	Earlier mentioned criterion.
17.	1975-76	NIRD	225.0	47.7	Earlier mentioned criterion.
18.	1976-77	NIRD	236.0	45.2	Earlier mentioned criterion.
19.	1977-78	Planning Commission	251.7	50.8	Rs. 741.60 p.c., c.e., p.a., (2,400 calories per day).
		IIPO	246.0	50.8	Rs. 780 p.c., c.e., p.a., 24 calories per day.
20.	1979-80	Planning Commission	259.6	50.7	Rs. 7.6 per person per month at current prices (2,400 calories per day).

p.c. = per capita, c.e. = consumer expenditure, p.a. = per annum.

3

Planning Poverty Removal: A National Perspective

Poverty is a curse hence removal of poverty was put on the priority in the development planning in India during 1951. The growth or development of the economy loses its meaning if there are no objectives of poverty removal. The approach or strategy may differ under different circumstances or people may differ in their course of action. It only goes to reflect divergences in the appreciation of the development process. The planning and its implementation has seen many shifts over a period of time due to the past experiences as well as the changing needs of the day. The change in approach has been very sharp since the mid-seventies and the poverty removal has been on priority agenda of all the governments, both at the Centre as well as at the state level.

It was felt that poverty is the consequence of lack of economic growth, which was due to the conditions prevailing during the British Raj. Hence lot of emphasis was given to structural and institutional modifications in the economy through direct intervention by the state in the initial phase covering the period from 1951 to 1965. Industrialization of the economy was considered as an indispensable means to accelerate the tempo of economic growth and poverty removal. Land reforms and agrarian restructing were considered necessary to help mobilize the agricultural sector for enhanced growth and overall development. It was based on the assumption that economic growth sets in motion, the dynamic changes in a stagnant economy. The most significant change that economic growth creates is in widening the range of choice that is available to an economy often literally over life and death questions (Chowdhary, 1991).

Economic planning was tailored to the compulsions of a mixed economy that the country opted for the roles of private and public sectors were defined and delineable so than both could contribute for putting the economy on firm trajectory of growth and transformation. The public sector was assigned the key role of developing heavy industries and building up of infrastructure, whereas the private sector was encouraged to raise output levels in agriculture and consumer goods. The public sector was expected to perform the role of the promoter of capital accumulation. The private sector was expected to regulate through various measure so that the broader social purpose could be served and growth monopolies checked.

The Second Five-Year Plan 1956 following words "the pattern of development and the structure of socio-economic relations should be so planned that they result not only in appreciable increases in national income and employment but also greater equality in incomes and wealth. Major decisions regarding production, distribution, consumption and investment — and in fact all significant socio-economic relationships-must be made by agencies informed by social purposes". (Second Five Year Plan, G.O.I).

It was envisaged that industrialization would absorb rural surplus labour in non-agricultural occupations and raise incomes and standard of living of the workers. Land reforms were expected to raise the income and consumption level of deprived sections of the rural population. Thus benefiting them through an axiomatic 'trickle down' mechanism. Fiscal policies, social securities for health and education as well as some technology development etc. were supposed to give impetus to the poverty removal mechanism.

It was also assumed that such an approach would bring a change in social institutes and the caste system etc.

However, it was realized that the development outcome in the first decade (1951-1960) did not give the desired or expected results on the poverty removal front. In the face of population growth rate of 2.5 per cent, the annual growth rate achieved was mere 3.5 per cent against the targeted 5.0 per cent, this resulting in per capita income growth rate of mere 1 per cent per annum. This could hardly lift the poorer segments of the society. In fact, the inflationary pressure worsened the lot of the poor. Prices of coarse grain the main staple food of the poorer sections of the society saw a sharper increase in comparison to the other types of grains, the economic growth proved detrimental in the sense that it led to concentration of income, wealth and power in fewer hands, mainly due to the growth of the big business houses in India (Mahalonobis Committee Report Vol. I).

As far as land reforms are concerned, the first phase was by and large, successful. The Zamindari System was abolished, thus the role of intermediaries (such as Zamindars and Jagirdars) was minimized, within a few years after Independence. This made the actual tillers, the owners of the land. They were involved in as much as 40 per cent of the cultivated area. These reforms could not be successfully implemented in some parts of India like those in north Bihar, where Zamindars continue to prosper and giving land on lease to the tillers. In successful areas, the land reforms have provided a major incentive for investment, growth and development. During the second round of reforms, the imposed ceiling on land holdings could not be much successful and the inequality in the distribution of holdings, persisted (Rao, 1991). Due to such factors, the development planning could not make a significant dent on poverty removal in the country. Pt. Jawaharlal Nehru expressed his distress and anguish in the following words.

> "Keeping in view the problem faced and the progress made, the Planning Commission also came into action to solve the problem of poverty in India. The perspective division of the commission (PPD, 1974) produced a document, which for the first time, highlighted and

quantified the magnitude of absolute poverty. This report pointed out that an annual rate of growth of 7 percent per annum sustained over the decade 1965-75 would be needed to give the poorest, three deciles nutritionally adequate diet (for this, the monthly consumption expenditure per capita was Rs 15 in 1960-61). Increase in aggregate national product was projected to be large enough to allow for some increase in the incomes at all levels after providing for necessary investment and some redistribution to the poor groups. The methods of this redistribution were not spelt out but were assumed to be entirely feasible. The document pointed out that a large number of people live in remote areas isolated from main stream of the economy. Also, much of the rural economy is loosely integrated with the growing sectors of the economy. All these and related factors had to be considered in the strategy for removal of poverty. A large group of landless labourers, small and marginal farmers as well as the under employment coupled with minimal mobility are the other factors that act as stumbling blocks in the automatic improvement of the income of the entire population plight of a greater proportion of the population, thus will remain static or the rate of improvement plight of a greater proportion of the population, thus, will remain static or the rate of improvement will be to slow, unless specific steps are taken to deal with this problem. Around one-fifth of the population is assumed to fall in this category (PDD, 1974)".

A working group, set up by the Government of India in 1962 suggested a consumption expenditure norm of Rs. 20 per month per capita (in terms of 1960-61 prices). This amount was considered bare minimum to meet the basic needs of a person. It assumed free education, free health care facilities as well as subsidy on urban housing. However, no specific criterion was used to justify this specification and was merely based on arbitrary judgement (Rudra, 1974).

This situation continued in the Third and Fourth Five Year Plans as no specific departure from the first two plans was suggested to deal with the mass poverty directly. The third plan did envisage to reduce the gap between the higher and the lower income and also to raise the level of the minimum (Third Five Year Plan, G.O.I.). The Plan envisaged the extension of the rural works programme. The Fourth Five Year Plan laid stress on removal of poverty. Through implementation of these plans, a reasonable level of per capita income may be attained in 10 years time period. The Fourth Five-Year plan envisaged that the consumption standards of the poor would remain unduly low in the absence of special efforts to alter the existing pattern of the distribution of income. This fourth plan assigned a bigger role to the agricultural growth in India's development process. Experience of the droughts of 1965-66 and 1966-67 prompted the formulation of technology based agricultural strategy.

The Fifth Five Year Plan gave impetus to the poverty alleviation programme through a direct interventionist strategy at the macro level. The minimum needs programme (MNP) was initiated during the period. It had two main components, viz improvement of the basic infrastructure like roads and drinking water, and providing the facilities for fulfilling the basic needs like education and health care. The MNP laid stress on human resource development through improvement in their productive capacity. This plan postulated that modifications in production structure, coupled with the above two components and price stability would enable the bottom 40-50 percent of the poor sections of the society to improve their standard of living. The plan formulated two variants of GDP growth viz, 6.5 and 5.5 percent. The farmer was expected to eliminate the decline in the average level of consumption of the first three deciles altogether, while the latter would not enable the top three deciles to maintain their consumption levels. This Plan laid stress on both energy sector and the agricultural sector so as meet the basic requirements of food and infrastructure. The plan strategy, however, had to be recasted due to Oil Crisis of 1973 as well as crop failures during 1972 and 1973 due to adverse climatic conditions. But this plan could highlighted the stark truth that poverty removal was predicated on: (a) a high rate of economic growth, particularly the agricultural component, and (b) modifications in the production structure.

Next came the Sixth Five Year Plan (1980-85) and the target group-oriented approach for removal of poverty was launched. But at the same time, it was indicated that seeing the magnitude of the task, it couldn't be accomplished in a short period of five years. On the basis of the National Sample Survey of Household consumer expenditure, it was observed that nearly 50 per cent of the Indian population was living below poverty line continuously over a long period (Sixth Five Year Plan, G.O.I.). Several programme were launched to meet the objective of poverty alleviation. Prominent among them were, the IRDP, NREP, TRYSEM and some other supplementary schemes. The targets of poverty reduction were kept as 30 per cent by 1984-85 and to less than 10 per cent by the end of 1986.

The first phase of India's economic growth represents an effort of transition from agrarian to the modern economic growth. To put the economy on rails, emphasis was laid on industrialization and institutional restructuring. To meet the objectives of social equality and growth, the second phase focused on technology based agricultural growth. In the third phase, priority was food and fuel sectors with an aim of economic growth and poverty removal. Direct intervention of the state became the main strategy for poverty alleviation. During the first four decades of independence, India has witnessed a concrete improvement and gains on the economy front, despite several constraints and ups and downs due to various reasons [Economic Survey, G.O.I 1991]. The national income registered an increase of 4.2 percent compound annual during the First Three Five Year Plans but came down to 2.7 percent in the next decade ending 1974-75. However, it again improved during the next decade or so *i.e.* 1975-76 to 1988-89 by registering an all time high of five per cent.

Per capita growth also experienced ups and downs. It was 1.9 percent during 1950-54, came down to 0.2 percent during 1965-74 again rose to 2.6 percent annual from 1975-76 onwards, to reach 3.4 percent in the eighties. During the later part, the economy saw a significant growth. A broad and diversified industrial development and self-sufficiency in food production are the highlights of this era. This has helped in saving foreign exchange especially in the food sector. A structural change, as reflected in the sectoral contribution to aggregate growth, has taken place in the economy. India has been able to successfully avert large-scale famines despite droughts, floods etc. It was mainly due to an effective public distribution system and availability of reserve food stocks. Though all this has strengthened and imparted resilience to the economy but still abysmal poverty persists in various regions and classes of the society. Everybody from policy planners to economists and the politicians agree that the problem of poverty has not been solved satisfactory in the country. It is also acknowledged and all are aware that the persistence of poverty and marginalization of the poor has the potential to nullify the very process of economic and social development.

Main cause behind all the problems related to poverty seems to be the colonial rule in India for over 200 years. During that period, hunger, malnutrition, illiteracy and deprivation stalked the country. A series of dietary surveys conducted by the Indian council of Medical Research during the period 1935-48 revealed that about one-fourth of the households were undernourished (Sukhatme, 1961). The Famine Inquiry Commission put this figure to 30 percent but argued that this much proportion of the poor were Hungry even in normal times (Famine Inquiry Commission, 1945). Since, most of the Indian population dwells in villages.

The condition of rural masses was appalling. Living conditions of an average Indian was portrayed by Vera Anstey who says, "*in many parts of India, it is fatally easy just to maintain life. A handful of rice, a cotton rag, a rural hut and dung cakes (for fuel) constitute the only necessities* (Anstey, 1952)".

After attaining the freedom, India has focused a special attention on the poor and the poverty alleviation. Because of this, the poor have started realizing that they are being counted and some help may come at sometime. They may not have received much help but have been subjected to several sophisticated head counts (Sen, 1974).

Several economists, statisticians, nutritionists as well as NGO's and independent research workers have investigated the problem of poverty. They have considered Rs. 20.00 (in terms of 1960-61 prices) per capita as the cut-off poverty line. The debate and controversy of the early seventies are two well known to bear repetition. The methodological problems involved in the debate are relevant even today. The empirical measurement of poverty is mostly based on the NSS data. The validity of this data has been questioned by many (Tyagi, 1990, Vaidyanathan, 1986). In the absence of any other database, the NSS data continues to be used. Ahluwalia (1978, 1986, 1990) found a statistically significant inverse relationship between rural poverty and agricultural performance for India as a whole as well as at State level. However, due to some other factors, the increase in the incidence of poverty was observed to be independent of variations in agricultural production per head. Ahluwalia's results and observations on the effect of agricultural growth on poverty have been critically examined and questioned by several economists. Griffin and Ghosh (1979) argue that during the period 1960-61 to 1973-74, there was no significant relationship between rural poverty and agricultural production at the state level, but Mundle (1984 a,b) has supported Ahluwalia's relationship on the basis of state level data. According to him, the growth and decline in agricultural sector in the two states Punjab and Bihar, respectively has a direct impact on poverty in these two states during the period 1963-64 to 1973-74.

Two more explanatory variables were added by Saith (1981), which were, a consumer price index and a time trend to the agricultural growth dependent inter-temporal variations in poverty. He pointed out that in India rural poverty is directly related to price variable and inversely to the agricultural production variable. In addition, it is directly related to the time trend. On this basis, he has shown a tendency to rise overtime after taking into account, the influence of price and production fluctuations. Gaiha (1987, 1989) has shown that the rural poverty and agricultural production were inversely related while, the effect of the latter in some cases, especially at the state level, was either weak or absent. The effect of price fluctuations, on the other hand was consistently strong and often decisive. This leads to the conclusion that the consumer price stabilization has a key role in anti-poverty strategy. Ghosh (1989) has further demonstrated that higher relative price of food grains/ agricultural products vis-à-vis manufacturing has poverty increasing impact. Similarly, Srinivasan (1986) pointed out that the trend value of gross output of agricultural grew a little faster, the value added component barely kept pace with population growth. On the ground, he rejected the "trickle down" hypothesis of Ahluwalia.

Chakravarty (1991) has argued that in general the incidence of rural poverty is much lower in states that have shown higher rates of growth in food grain production. According to him there is a close inverse correlation between growth in food production and incidence of poverty on a state wise basis, although there might have been other factors in operation. Narain (1986) postulated a relationship between the percentage of population below poverty line and the level of net domestic product in agriculturre per head of rural population, the level of food grains prices and the general time trend. He found a negative relationship between poverty and food prices. He also found a mildly declining time trend. Narain thought that agricultural performance and time was relevant in explaining temporal changes in poverty through regression analysis. He tried to expand Ahluwalia's specification by including nominal prices of commodities consumed by rural poor as an explanatory variable. Among the factors that Dharam Narain had in mind were the employments generated through binding of socio-economic overheads in rural areas, support to traditional cottage and village industries, growth of tertiary sector in rural areas resulting from agricultural development at an unprecedented pace, land reforms, development of cooperative institutions and growth in health, education and other sectors. He attached maximum importance to the land reforms of 1950's. Perhaps, because of this, he used 'Time' as an explanatory variable after logarithmic transformation (Desai and Mellor, 1986).

One of the major factors for persistence of rural poverty has been the failure of the economy to grow fast. Recently the growth rate has clocked 5 percent and it has been capital intensive. Employment generation has decelerated as a consequence of this during the earlier years; the employment grew at a rate of 2.2 per cent but the labour population at about 2.5 per cent per year, thus leading to unemployment backlog. The growth rate of employment was a meager 1.5 per annum during eighties. The situation in the organized sector was much better with an employment growth rate of 5.1 percent during early 1960's but 2.4 percent during 1983-88.

A declining trend in employment elasticity with respect of GDP growth in recent years has been more pronounced in the private sector. Total employment in the private sector was -0.07 percent as against 1.73 per cent in organized sector and 2.54 per cent in the public sector during the period 1981-87. In manufacturing sector, the employment grew in public sector (3.6 percent) while it decelerated in the private sector to -0.46 percent. In trade, the respective growth rates of employment have been 2.29 and .06% respectively for the public and private sectors in the recent years there has been a steeply declining employment content of output. In earlier period, out of 3.5 percent in long term economic growth, about 2 per cent was contributed by the employment growth and 1.5 per cent by output growth per worker. The recent years have witnessed a spurt in growth at the rate of 5 per cent per annum. However, the employment content of this growth rate has been 1.85 percent and the productivity growth content more than 3 percent (Rao, 1991).

An important factor in aggravating rural poverty is the iniquitous agrarian structure. In rural society, the asset ownership is highly in favour of the richer sections. The land and tenancy reforms introduced in seventies have been half-hearted in implementation and inadequate in content (Chakravarty, 1990). Absentee landlordism, various types of tenancy arrangements and the interlocking of factor markets have further accentuated the rural poverty. Landlessness and inequality in operational holdings have deteriorated overtime. The distribution of assets is highly biased in favour of the top three deciles of the rural society. There has not been any change in assets ownership during the sixties. The asset of 'poor' household consists only of their huts, a few household goods and some livestock (Sixth Five-Year Plan, 1980-85).

Considering those poor households are those with less than Rs. 1000.00 of assets (as per 1961 price level), percentage of such households increased from 30 to 35 per cent during 1961 to 1971.

The technology based agricultural development has enabled India to achieve and sustain a growth rate of food grains higher than the population growth rate. This is supported by the Government policies and incentives like support price, subsidies and provision of credit at the concessional rates etc. However, this has led to inter-regional and inter-personnel disparities in different regions and sections of the rural society such as land owners, landless labourers, large and medium farmers vis-à-vis small and marginal farmers. Benefits of new technology and increased output benefited the rich and progressive farmers in progressive states like Punjab, Haryana parts of western U.P. and Andhra Pradesh (Bhalla, 1987; Rao 1991). Poverty among the landless increased over the period. The high growth in population rate has been major cause of poverty and unemployment and the population growth rate as assumed in First Five Year Plan looks ridiculous.

The relationship between population growth and the incidence of poverty have been investigated by Walle (1981). He found significant adverse effects of population growth on poverty inspite of the favourable effects of agricultural output and real wages rates. He based his analysis on the period 1959-60 to 1970-71, by pooling together, both cross-section and time series data of different states, Planning Commission document assumed that during the period 2001-2006 A.D., the birth rate will fall to 25 per thousand in comparison to 30 per 1000 in 1981-86, and that the countries population will exceed one billion mark by 2000 AD. The UN projections indicate that India's population will be between 1300 to 1600 million by the year 2025. Various populations projective have put the population of India as around 1800 million by 2150 AD (UN, 1989).

High level of population growth has lot of bearing on Indian economy hence the utmost priority should be to reduce the rate of population growth, thereby reducing the negative effect of population growth on economic growth. The family welfare programme have mostly focused on mechanical and clinic approach and almost ignored the social, cultural and economic aspects of the programme. The major emphasis through Government run programme is on promoting small family norms, sterilization and propagation of various contraceptives measures. Experience has shown that the reduction in population growth is very much influenced by the social and economic level of the group. For this, increase in literacy rate, especially of women, child welfare in terms of nutrition and health care and above all, community participation in family welfare programme are the main components, which can help in reducing the present population growth rate. Hence well designed. Strategies are needed for tackling this burning problem.

In the rural society, common property resources (CPR's) are an important part of life. These include, community forests, futures, water resources and tanks etc. These contribute much to the income generation, employment and sustaining the life of the village poor. It has been estimated that in terms of income, the CPR's contributed about Rs. 530 to Rs. 830 per family per year in terms of income in different areas (Jodha, 1986).

Despite the importance of CPR's in the life of the rural masses, their productivity as well as the area in declining, thus contributing to the increase in poverty. The area under CPR's has decreased from 63 to 23 percent during the last three decades and large-scale privatization has also taken place during this period of time. The privatization was done to help the poor but 49 to 86 percent of these fell in the hands of the rich in different parts of the country. Also, in many cases, the poor could not maintain and develop these CPR's due to lack of resources with the result that they had to leave these. Thus, the rural poor lost a significant part of their source of livelihood through decline of CPR's. This loss could not be compensated by privatization of the CPR's that were given to the rural poor. The situation, thus call for a greater attention to CPR's as a part of the anti-poverty strategy (Jodha, 1986).

The denudation of forests deprived the rural poor of his easy access to fuel and fodder along with resultant environmental degeneration and the associated hazards.

The anti-poverty interventionist strategy is aimed at assisting the households below the poverty line through appropriate package of technologies, services and asset transfers. Broadly, there have been three approaches, viz;

i) the minimum needs programme (MNP),

ii) the household oriented programme of income generation through assets and skill endowment and direct wage employment through public works; and

iii) programme for special areas to counter endemic poverty caused by hostile agro climatic conditions and degeneration of the eco-system.

The MNP, introduced in 1974-75, consisted of two distinct activities, viz;

i) human resources development activities like elementary and adult education, health, drinking water, rural housing and nutrition, and

ii) area development activities such as roads village electrification. The major objective was to raise the productive capacity of the community as a whole.

The other programme aimed at improving the economic conditions of the individuals in a direct manner. The main objective of these programmes is to provide wage employment on a large scale in the rural areas to landless labourers and the marginal farmers during the slack season. Development of durable community assets was an important component of these programme. Food for work is also a significant feature of the programme. This also ensured the improvement in the nutrition status of these rural poor. Similarly, the creation or provision of wide variety of community assets is expected to raise the levels of living in the rural areas. Thus, the two sets of programme mentioned above are as such complimentary with each other to meet the objective of upliftment of the poor.

In 1980-81, the NREP (National Rural Employment Programme) was initiated with the objective of providing supplementary employment opportunities to those selling work during lean periods. A target of 300-400 million man-days of employment per annum was set. NREP also envisaged the creation of community assets for continuing benefits to the poor and for strengthening the rural infrastructure. Another programme, RLLEGP (Rural Landless Labour Employment Guarantee Programme) was launched in 1983 with the objective of providing guaranteed employment to at least one member of a landless labour household for upto 100 days in a year and the target was fixed at 300 million man-days a year.

The asset endowment programme IRDP (Integrated Rural Development Programme) initiated in 1978-79 has become a major national programme over the year. The programme is designed to create self-employment opportunities on regular basis to enable the beneficiaries to cross the poverty line on a permanent basis. The programme covers activities in primary, secondary and tertiary sectors and financing is done through a mix of government subsidies and institutional credit. This programme has two sub-programmes, namely, TRYSEM and DWCRA. The former was targeted for the rural youth while the latter was a meant for the rural women. During Sixth Plan, two major development programmes were DPAP (Drought Prone Area Programme) and DPP. These programme aimed at restoration of ecological balance of various areas through soil and moisture conservation, development and management of irrigation potential, afforestation, checking of further desertification by sand-dune, stabilization and shelter belt plantations, restructuring of cropping system and development of livestock resources. These measures aimed at increasing the productive potential of the areas and enhancing the self-employment opportunities in the long run.

At the National level, it is claimed that the antipoverty programmes have made a substantial impact on poverty. Various poverty-alleviating programme were evaluated by various economists and research agencies (Rao and Rath, 1985 and Rangaswamy, 1988). Though, conflicting evidence has come to light but all do not deny the positive role of these programmes in poverty alleviation.

The 7th Plan claims a sharp fall in the poverty ratio between 1977-78 and 1983-84. The main reason for this welcome trend is the higher rate of economic growth and the increased agricultural production. Sixth Plan also saw the expansion of the IRDP, which was extended to cover all the blocks in the country, and the NREP that strived for providing employment in rural works RLEGP also helped in providing employment during the last two years of the Plan. (Seventh Five Year Plan). The estimates of the Planning Commission pointed to a further decline in rural poverty to around 28 percent in 1989-90. However, many leading economists in the country challenged these estimates and opined that this reduction in poverty is procedural as it is a direct consequence of the pro-rata adjustment of the NSS consumption distribution estimates (Minhas 1987, 1989 and 1991).

Minhas et. al. (1991) conducted a detailed state-wise analysis based on consumer expenditure in the rural areas as obtained from the NSS. They say that a larger proportion of the rural people live below the poverty line than the number estimated by the Planning Commission They have shown that the massive reduction in the incidence of poverty between 1983 and 1987-88 as reported by Planning Commission in 1990 is largely a consequence of the particular statistical artifacts used by it and the extent of real reduction in poverty incidence is indeed rather small. By computing the data on incidence of poverty in 1987-88 through appropriate price adjustment at All India level, the level of poverty comes to 44.8 and 36.5 percent, in rural and urban India, respectively rather than 32.7 and 19.4 percent as reported by the Planning Commission.

Minhas et. al. (1991) summarized that according to their preferred aggregated All India estimates, which allow for specific variation in prices relevant to the poor population in each of the states, the incidence of poverty comes to about 48.7 and 37.8 percent for rural and urban societies, respectively.

Conflicting evidence about the efficacy of anti-poverty programme has accumulated over the years in the country. While some studies have highlighted the success aspects, others have demonstrated the failure of the package to meet the objectives. In India, the poverty debate is an on going process. The experience of many countries shows that initially, anti-poverty programme may have a tickle-up rather than trickle down impact (Adelma and Robinson, 1978).

In Indian context, the growth and social justice are complementary and an exclusive emphasis on either is likely to generate contradiction, pressures and difference of opinion. Only the sustained economic growth can ensure the eradication of poverty in the long run but the incidence of severe poverty calls for public intervention. However, the direct public intervention and anti-poverty programme have their own limitations. Even the Planning Commission has acknowledged this. At the same time, identifying the limiting factors of the higher growth rate, some medium term, more direct means of reducing the incidence of poverty in the stage of transition would have to be employed (Sixth Five Year Plan, 1981-85).

The national policy in India aims at ensuring a higher rate of economic growth on sustained basis. It is estimated that at the present rate of population growth, India would need to have a rate of growth of around 12-14 percent per annum to eradicate the poverty within the next two decades (Gupta, 1989). However, such a high growth rate is not attainable in near future. Hence a direct attack on poverty was perceived to be necessary. But at most of the times, such anti-poverty programmes are transitory, redistributive schemes that do not lead to the creation of permanent income generating assets for the poor. (Krishnan, 1990). Only the sustained economic growth and sound public policies can ensure the raising up of the entitlements of the poor, otherwise there is the possibility that those who are pulled above the poverty line, may slide back into the poverty again. A strong case has been made for raising the entitlements of the poor through asset accessibility. Dharam Narain who has emphasized has propounded the asset endowment approach neatly that the effectively implemented land redistribution policy is the basic requirement for a broad based rural development strategy (Narain, 1990).

One of the most important components in the poverty removal strategy is the targeting of the deserving poor. The proper and efficient selection of the right beneficiary would reduce the costs, but even more important is the inclusion of the non-poor, which means denying the genuine beneficiary, the benefits of the programme.

There are some unavoidable constraints like information constraints, yet there is a lot of scope to correct it (Sen, 1992). It is very important that despite the constraints, poverty removal or alleviation programme should ensure the proper use and distribution of resources so that it could enhance social output and activity.

4

Incidence of Poverty

An attempt has been made in this chapter to work out the incidence of poverty. A large number of studies have been conducted to estimate the incidence of poverty in and across the country. Most of these have either been done at the All India or state levels. Very few studies deal with the incidence of poverty at the regional or sub-regional level.

Incidence of poverty has rarely been worked out along with income, assets and consumption inequalities. Changes in the levels of poverty cannot be appreciated adequately unless these are linked to the impact of agrarian transformation and economic development on structure variable like income, consumption and assets. The need for poverty studies at the regional or sub-regional level is self-explanatory. Such studies assume significance in view of variation in attitude, climate and living conditions and as such provide fresh analytical insights into the dynamics of poverty.

Against this backdrop the chapter seeks to explore the link between poverty and backwardness.

Some of the studies use the country-specific poverty norm for working out incidence of poverty at the state level. A few notable such estimates are available for Jammu and Kashmir also. Notable among these are:

Gupta et al. (1983), Planning Commission, Government of India (1986), Gupta and Joshi (1990) and Minhas et al.

(1991). While the first study has been carried out for the period 1960-61 to 1973-74, the Planning Commission study utilised the results of the 32nd round (1978 revised) and 38th round (provisional) NSS expenditure surveys to work out the poverty ratio's.

Gupta, et. al. worked out the poverty lines for different states by All India calorie norm and by estimating separately the calorie norm at the regional level. NSS consumption expenditure surveys for 1972-73 and 1977-78, which provide information on consumption of food, form the basis of these exercises. Minhas and Jain (1990) have worked out state specific cost of living indices for the entire rural population and middle band of rural population. With the help of these indices poverty lines and poverty ratio's have been computed for each state (Minhas et. al. 1991). Using country specific calorie norm Gupta and Joshi (1990) have estimated the calorie content of monthly per capita expenditure while calculating the poverty lines, the norm of 2,200 calorie per consumer unit per day has been used and the poverty ratio's were then worked out. Following Dandekar (1980), Gupta et al. (1983) used a general indicator *i.e.*, proportion of expenditure on food for measuring poverty. People spending 80 percent or more of their consumption expenditure on food were identified as poor. They estimated poverty with this method for 1972-73, estimates of poverty based on the above studies are presented in the appendix II.

METHODOLOGY

For computing the incidence of poverty at a point of time in a particular region a region-specific poverty line (Z) and a region-specific distribution of population by income or expenditure are needed. A person with income or consumption less then Z is classified as poor. Z can be estimated by employing any one of the following alternatives:

i) Using the country-specific poverty line as a substitute for the regional poverty line;

ii) Using the country-specific calorie norm as a proxy for the region-specific calorie norm;

iii) Adjusting country-specific poverty line with the help of a region-specific price deflator;

iv) Using the proportion of expenditure on food as a norm for identifying the poor;

v) Estimating poverty line from the regional consumption expenditure and associated calorie content of food by estimating separately the calorie requirement at the regional level considering age-sex-activity wise distribution of population.

Recommendation of the Expert Group on estimation of proportion and number of poor (Perspective Planning Division, Planning Commission, Govt. of India, July, 1993).

Rural Poverty Line

The All-India rural poverty line of Rs. 49 at 1973-74 prices is taken as the base. This is adjusted to reflect the observed differences in the rural cost of living across states. State wise Consumer Price Index for Agricultural Labourers (CPIAL) for food and general indices with 1960-61 as the base year are available. Based on weights of food and general indices of each state, the implicit indices of non-food items for the state have been worked out. Having obtained food and non-food indices for each state the combined consumer price index is obtained using the consumption pattern of the people around the poverty line at the national level for 1973-74. The latter group of population contained the poverty norm in 1973-74 and closely corresponds to the 40 to 60 percent fractile group. The All-India consumption pattern of food and non-food has been obtained from the NSS report relating to 1973-74 and used as weighting diagram. The state-specific consumer price indices thus derived are adjusted for the base year price differentials using Fishers rural cost of living index reflecting price differentials across the states for 1960-61 as adopted by Minhas from Chatterjee and Bhattacharya. Given these adjusted state-specific consumer price indices for 1973-74, the state specific poverty line for 1973-74 corresponding to the All-India poverty lines is derived. For the year 1977-78, 1983 and 1987-88 the Consumer Price Index for Agricultural Workers are available for four groups of commodities namely 'food', 'fuel and light', 'clothing and footwear' and 'miscellaneous' with base 1960-61 = 100. Accordingly, the state specific price indices for rural areas in respect of each state are worked out using price of the above four groups. The All-India consumption pattern of people around the poverty line for the above four broad commodity groups in 1973-74 has been used as the weighting diagram for constructing state specific price indices for the rural population for the three NSS survey years *i.e.* 1977-78, 1983 and 1987-88. The state specific poverty line for 1973-74 are then updated for the years, *i.e.* 1977-78, 1983 and 1987-88 by moving them the state specific Consumer price Index obtained for these three years as discussed above.

Updating Poverty Line

Z = Rs. 46.59 Given P L at 1973-74 prices.

1. Used adjusted CPIAL.
2. CPIAL available at 1960-61 prices, changed base of this series to 1973-74.
3. Worked out the adjusted CPIAL for reference year by using base year consumption distribution *i.e.* 1973-74, 28th round NSS.

4) CPIAL for 1995-96 was not available, so we increased it in the same proportion as in the previous year.
5) With this adjusted CPIAL, we updated Z, which works out to be Rs. 242 for 1995-96.

In the present study, we have used four criterions - two concepts of income and two of expenditure. Farm business income (FBI), total net returns (TNR) are the income concepts. Monthly per capita total expenditure and monthly per man day total expenditure are the consumption expenditure concepts. The meaning of these concepts is provided in appendix are the consumption expenditure concepts. The meaning of these concepts is provided in the appendix of this chapter.

To get the distribution of population along the above criteria, Jammu Tehsil was divided into two-relief regions namely Plain region and Kandi region. All the villages on the right of Ranbir canal constitute plain region and villages on the left bank of the canal forms Kandi region.

Variations in regions are reflected in variations in land use patterns, irrigation, infrastructural facilities, level of state intervention, occupational and consumption pattern, which are very important to under, stand the dynamics of poverty. In order to reduce the levels of heterogeneity on account of these variables and make the sampling frame as homogeneous as possible, regions serve as a reliable basis of classification.

Location of villages in the above clusters was marked from the maps published by survey of India. Cluster wise classification of villages was done on the basis of their percentage of their population ranging from 0-25, 25-50, 50-75 and 75+. Villages in the same proportion were selected from the above four groups, to make the sample unbiased in terms of population size villages. 16 villages were selected as the second sampling unit. A uniform percentage of the households from all the strata within all the clusters was obtained. In all 200 households were finally selected for the integrated survey. These households were classified region-wise into agricultural labour; marginal, small, medium and large farmers. An integrated pre-tested questionnaire was canvassed to collect information regarding:

1) Income from agricultural activities;
2) Income from allied agricultural activities;
3) Income from other sources;

4) Levels and structure of assets;

5) Consumption expenditure per household per-month.

Various indices of measuring poverty have been proposed (see Barooah, 1992 and Sharma et. al. 1989 for review of those indices). The most commonly used index of poverty is the Head Count Ratio. Another method called Income-gap ratio measures poverty shortfalls of all the poor's income from poverty line (Z). Sen (1976) proposed an alternative measure "P" which takes care of the limitations of (H) and (I) and combines them as P = H {[I + (1 - I)] GC}. In the present study, we employed Hand P to measure Incidence of Poverty. The formulae used:

1) $H = (q/n) \times 100$ **where:**

	H	=	Head Count Ratio
	q	=	Number of people below poverty line
	n	=	Total Population

2) $P_s = q\,(1 - (y/z) + (y/z)\,GC)$ **where**

	P_s	=	Sen's measure of poverty
	q	=	Head Count Ratio
	Y	=	mean Income/Consumption of the poor
	z	=	Poverty Line
	GC	=	Gini co-efficient of the income/ consumption distribution of the poor

The value of Gini Co-efficient of Income/Consumption distribution of the poor have been computed by the following formula:

$$GC = 1 + (1+q) - (2/q^2 z) \square (q + - i)\, Y_i$$

where

GC = Gini co-efficient of the Income/ Consumption distribution of the poor

Z = Mean Income/Consumption of the poor

q = Number of people below poverty line

Y_i = Income/Consumption of the ith poor person

SAMPLE FEATURES

Age of the respondents; educational level of the respondents; male, female and total literary; land; irrigation; input structure; returns from farm activities; returns from livestock and other sources; total net returns from all sources; level and structure of assets and consumption across the size categories of the sampled households and the regions have been presented in Tables 4.1 to 4.10 as a prelude to the analysis of the incidence of poverty and income/consumption/assets concentration. These factors have a direct bearing on the incidence of poverty and inequality of income/consumption/assets. These features are briefly described as under.

Average of the respondent for the sample as whole turns out to be 44.82 yrs. while as it is 44.99 yrs. in the Kandi region and 44.66 yrs. in the Plain region, whereas in case of categories, large farmers respondent age turns out to be highest *i.e.* 54.41 yrs. overall, whereas Kandi large farmer respondent and plain farmer respondent age turns out to be 51 yrs. and 56.8 yrs. respectively (see Table 4.1).

More than 70 percent of the respondents in the entire sample are educated. Large farmers record the highest literacy among the respondents. Large farmers record the highest size of family in both the regional and the regions as a whole. Agriculture labourers, contrary to the general belief, record the lowest size of the family. Average size of the family works out to be 5.950 for the sample as a whole if we convert the number of family members into consuming units as suggested by the Planning Commission and Indian Council of Medical Research for rural population. The total sample population of 1190 male, female and children has been converted into 'Standard Consumer Units' or adult man value by applying the 'scale of co-efficient' suggested by the Indian Council of Medical Research. In the present study by applying the above-mentioned reference the total consumer units have been worked out to be 1218. Large farmers record the highest size of consuming units average size of consuming units work out to be 6.14 for the sample as a whole (See Table 4.3 and 4.4).

Both male and female literacy are more in the plain region *i.e.*; 40.39 percent and 32.08 percent respectively while among the categories medium farmers record the highest percentages *i.e.* 53.84 percent in case of male literacy and large farmers record the highest *i.e.* 33.33 percent (see Table 4.5 and 4.6). The plain region record the highest literacy of 36.49 percent and among the categories the medium farmers records the highest literacy of 42.59 per cent. State's literacy rate is 26.67%age. (1981 census). Sex ratio for the sample turns out to be 882.53. Among the regions, Plain belt records higher sex ratio (*i.e.*; 892.22) than the Kandi region (868.58). Large farmers record sex ratio (*i.e.*; 960) in the Kandi region and medium farmer record (1000) sex ratio in the plain region. Medium farmers record highest sex ratio of 914.06, which is the highest among the categories. Large farmers record the lowest sex ratio (818.18) among the categories (see Table : 4.8).

Average size of the ownership holding works out to be 3.16, 218 and 2.17 acres in the kandi region, plain region and region as a whole Average size of the holding for the samples as a whole is slightly greater than the state average. Per capita availability of land is more in case of the kandi region than the plain region, this is because, while categorizing we had taken double the land for each category (Ref. Table : 4.9 and 4.10).

Plain region is irrigated by the Ranbir Canal whereas farmers in the Kandi region, are virtually dependant on monsoon in summer and south westerly, which bring rain in winter 1995-96, the survey period was a normal period as far as monsoon and winter rainfall is concerned. Wheat is the dominant crops in both the regions during the rabbi season. Oil seeds, Pulses, Potatoes etc. are mainly grown during the Rabi season. Rice and Maize are the dominant crops of Plain and Kandi regions respectively are the main kharief crops. All the features of the cropping pattern of the sampled household are in conformity with the over and entire cropping pattern of the Jammu region.

Marginal holdings turn out to be labour intensive compared to large holdings. Large farmers use more fertilizers; manure, chemicals and bullock labour compared to the marginal farmers who spend more on implements, farm buildings and maintenance of equipments. Most of the items under variable costs are available either in the open market or government controlled marketing outlets where invariably cash in hand and access to these markets become the key requirements for their timely utilization provided a farmer is willing to make use of these outlets.

Greater use of human labour on marginal farms could be due to the lack of alternative employment avenues and consequent presence of unemployment or disguised unemployment. However, in the absence of any conclusive evidence nothing concrete can be inferred from this scenario.

Land is the most important asset in all the size classes (except agricultural labour) and the regions. It constitutes more than sixty percent of the total assets in these classes and regions and the sample as a whole. The percentage of land in the total assets turn out to be the highest in the large farmers among the size classes and in the Kandi among the regions. Next to land are the buildings. Both these assets together constitute more than 85% of the total assets in all sizes, classes/regions and the sample as a whole. Livestock constitute about 3 per cent of the total assets. Values of total assets per capita are positively related to scale among the regions and all the regions put together.

The distribution of the assets across the categories and the regions is thus in conformity with the distribution of assets in the state as a whole.

Expenditure on all the food items constitutes 74.52%, 71.25% and 72.80% of the total expenditure in the Kandi, Plain and Sample as a whole respectively. The percentages for agricultural labour, marginal farmer, small farmer, medium farmer and the large farmer classes in the sample as a whole turn out to be 72.50%, 72.24%, 74.08%, 74.50% and 66.90% respectively (see table 4.29).

Among the food items cereals account for the major share of expenditure and is positively associated with the scale across the regions and the sample as whole. Expenditure on cereals as a percentage of total expenditure on food and total expenditure on all items, work out to be: 37.97% and 28.29%; 37.90% and 27.01%; 37.94% and 27.62% in the Kandi region, Plain region and for the entire sample respectively. In absolute terms, Plain region among the regions and the large farmers among the size classes record the highest expenditure on cereals (see Table 4.11). The expenditure on: milk and milk products; pulses; edible oil; meat, fish and eggs; vegetables; processed food; sugar; salt; spices, beverages and fruits as a percentages of total expenditure on food and total expenditure on all items works out to be: 15.14% and 11.02%; 11.93% and 8.68%; 5.17% and 3.76%; 3.24% and 2.36%; 6.40% and 4.66%; 3.34% and 2.43%; 4.21% and 3.07%; 0.75% and 0.55%; 3.27% and 2.38%; 4.43% and 3.22%; 4.01% and 2.92% respectively in the entire sample (Ref. Table 4.12 to 4.22).

The plain areas among the regions and large farmers from the size classes record the highest expenditure on non-food items. Among the non-food items clothing, durable goods, miscellaneous goods and fuel and light are the most important items. Their percentage share in the total non-food expenditure turns out to be 25.31% (Clothing), 12.55% (Miscellaneous goods), 12.77% (Intoxicants), 10.30% (Durable goods) (ref. Table 4.23 to 4.28). We have ranked the regions and the size classes according to their respective scores in terms of indicators. The results have been presented in Table A and Table B. It is clear from these tables that the plain region emerged the most developed region among the regions and the large farmers more prosperous among the size classes.

INCIDENCE OF POVERTY

Given the exogenously defined poverty line the sampled population has been distributed according to the following criteria's to estimate the incidence of poverty :

1) Farm business income (FBI distribution).
2) Total net returns (TNR distribution).
3) Per-capita per month monthly total consumption expenditure;
4) Per consuming unit per month monthly total consumption expenditure.

Head-count and Sens (1976) methods have been used to estimate the incidence.

Employing Head Count Ratio to FBI distribution the incidence of poverty works out to be 62.22%, 49.42% and 55.71% in the Kandi region, Plain region and the Sample as a whole. The corresponding values of Sen.'s measure size upto 45.98%, 40.13% and 43.05%.

Incidence of poverty declines in all the regions and the total population if we concentrate on TNR distribution around 35% of the total sampled population lives below the poverty line (see Table 4.36). TNR distribution includes income from activities, livestock and other sources. Thus, it is clear that the incidence of poverty is more in those areas and households, which solely depend on farm activities for income. It also implies that along with the modernization of farm activities, diversification of the rural economy on the extensive scale is one of the necessary conditions for the removal of poverty.

Poverty according to the distribution of population by per capita per month total consumption expenditure is lower in the Plain region than the Kandi region. Head count ratio for the Kandi region, Plain region and sample as a whole turns out to be 41.88%, 29.91% and 35.71% respectively. The corresponding values for the Sen's measure work out to be 18.14%, 12.36% and 14.74% respectively. Compared to the TNR the poverty ratio's increases the region and sample as a whole. It means that some income is saved for capital accumulation, repayment of accumulated debt & debt services or lending money to people (which is normally not recorded in formal deeds) is another common mode of diversion. Purchase of tangible assets, particularly land, could be the third source of diversion.

The poverty scene undergoes a slight change for the worse if incidence is calculated from the distribution of population according to per consuming unit per month total consumption. Incidence increases in all the regions and sample as a whole (refer Table 4.36).

All the poverty ratios confirm the inference deduced from the ranking of the regions according to different performance indicators *i.e.* the more under developed a region higher the incidence of poverty.

The main findings of the preceding discussions are:

1) Large farmers record the highest size of the family and very low sex ratio. While the converse is true in case of agricultural labourers (Size of family).
2) Among the regions the Plain region record higher sex ratio than the Kandi region.
3) Size of ownership holding does not necessarily determine the level of education.
4) The average size of the holdings works out to be highest in the Kandi region.
5) The pressure on land is more acute in the Plain region as compared to other regions. The region is agriculturally more developed.

6) All the features of cropping and irrigation patterns in the Sampled region are in conformity with the overall cropping and irrigation patterns of the region.

7) Marginal holdings turn out to be labour intensive. Marginal farmers spend more on implements, farm buildings and maintenance of equipments. Large farmers use more of fertilizers, manure, chemicals and bullock labour.

8) Land is the most important asset across the size classes and the regions (except agricultural labourers). It constitutes more than 60% of the total assets held. Along with buildings the percentage goes as high as 80% of the total assets.

9) The Plain region is more developed region among the regions and the large farmers are the most prosperous among the size categories.

10) Among the food items cereals account for the major share of expenditure across the regions and size classes/categories. The Plain region among the regions and the large farmers from the size categories record the highest expenditure on the non-food items. The Plain region and the large farmers record the highest total expenditure per sampled household and per capita.

11) In the per capita consumption expenditure of the size classes agricultural labourers and marginal farmers are lagging behind the large farmer but not much behind the overall expenditure of the sample.

12) All the poverty ratio's confirm the inferences deduced from the ranking of the regions according to different indicators. The more under developed a region higher is the incidence of poverty.

Consumer Price Index for Agricultural Labourers

Base 1960-61 = 100

S. No.	*Years*	*Food Group*	*Fuel & Light*	*Clothing & Footwear*	*Miscell-aneous*
1.	1973-74	287	110	226	216
2.	1974-75	363	118	294	264
3.	1975-76	384	119	291	293
4.	1976-77	347	121	298	306
5.	1977-78	371	121	320	317
6.	1978-79	371	122	333	328
7.	1979-80	383	127	351	356
8.	1980-81	412	129	381	400
9.	1981-82	458	134	415	435
10.	1982-83	518	137	443	477
11.	1983-84	585	139	469	527
12.	1984-85	600	142	502	580
13.	1985-86	628	147	537	623
14.	1986-87	675	150	549	650
15.	1987-88	755	152	565	702
16.	1988-89	801	147	592	780
17.	1989-90	824	148	667	859
18.	1990-91	922	160	757	931
19.	1991-92	1032	162	902	1083
20.	1992-93	1137	163	974	1195
21.	1993-94	1287	164	1071	1331
22.	1994-95	1379	168	1304	1476
23.	1995-96	1471	172	1671	1609

Source: Labour Bureau, Shimla.

Consumer Price Index For Agricultural Labourers

Base 1973-74 = 100

S.No.	*Years*	*Food Group*	*Fuel & Light*	*Clothing & Footwear*	*Miscell-aneous*	*Average* (4 + 5 + 6)/3
1	2	3	4	5	6	3
1.	1974-75	126.48	107.27	130.08	122.22	119.85
2.	1975-76	133.79	108.18	128.76	135.64	124.19
3.	1976-77	120.90	110.00	131.85	141.66	127.84
4.	1977-78	129.26	110.00	141.59	146.76	132.78
5.	1978-79	129.26	110.90	147.34	151.85	136.69
6.	1979-80	133.44	115.45	155.31	164.81	145.19
7.	1980-81	143.55	117.27	168.58	185.18	157.01
8.	1981-82	159.58	121.81	183.62	201.38	168.93
9.	1982-83	180.48	124.54	196.02	220.83	180.46
10.	1983-84	203.83	126.36	207.52	243.98	192.62
11.	1984-85	209.05	129.09	222.12	268.52	206.57
12.	1985-86	218.81	133.63	237.61	288.42	219.88
13.	1986-87	235.19	136.36	242.92	300.92	226.73
14.	1987-88	263.06	138.18	250.00	325.00	237.72
15.	1988-89	279.09	133.63	261.94	361.11	252.23
16.	1989-90	287.10	134.54	295.13	397.68	275.78
17.	1990-91	321.25	145.45	334.95	431.02	303.80
18.	1991-92	359.58	147.27	399.11	501.38	349.25
19.	1992-93	396.16	148.18	430.97	553.24	377.46
20.	1993-94	448.43	149.09	473.89	616.20	413.06
21.	1994-95	480.48	152.72	576.99	680.55	470.08
22	1995-96	514.83	158.26	702.54	751.60	537.46

Calculated from the above Table.

Table 4.1

Age of the Respondents by the size classes of households and the regions

Size Category	*Kandi*	*Plain*	*Total*
Large	51.00	56.80	54.41
Medium	41.90	45.63	43.67
Small	47.40	46.76	47.26
Marginal	45.12	40.89	43.03
Landless	33.60	38.14	36.25
Total	**44.99**	**44.66**	**44.82**

Source: Field Survey.

Table 4.2

Educational level of the respondents by the size classes of households and the regions

Size Category	*Kandi*	*Plain*	*Total*
Large	71.42	80.00	6.47
Medium	47.61	68.42	7.50
Small	77.77	53.33	4.90
Marginal	72.60	76.92	4.68
Landless	60.00	71.42	6.66
Total	**68.00**	**72.10**	**70.00**

Source: Field Survey.

Table 4.3

Size of households by the size classes of households and the regions

Size Category	*Kandi*	*Plain*	*Total*
Large	7.00	9.200	8.294
Medium	5.809	6.421	6.100
Small	6.592	6.160	6.384
Marginal	5.350	5.256	5.303
Landless	4.40	4.571	4.500
Total	**5.58**	**6.05**	**5.950**

Source: Field Survey.

Table 4.4

Size of households (consumer units) by the size classes of households and the regions

Size Category	*Kandi*	*Plain*	*Total*
Large	8.214	9.480	8.958
Medium	5.904	6.563	6.217
Small	7.107	6.24	6.690
Marginal	5.465	5.30	5.383
Landless	4.02	4.814	4.483
Total	**6.121**	**6.159**	**6.14**

Source: Field Survey.

Table 4.5

Male literacy by the size classes of the households and the regions

Size Category	*Kandi*	*Plain*	*Total*
Large	29.411	37.931	34.782
Medium	45.833	60.714	53.846
Small	26.666	33.333	29.629
Marginal	28.301	36.000	32.038
Landless	20.000	37.500	30.769
Total	**30.555 40.397**	**37.293**	

Source: Field Survey.

Table 4.6

Female literacy by the size classes of households and the regions

Size Category	*Kandi*	*Plain*	*Total*
Large	25.000	38.095	33.333
Medium	23.333	34.615	28.571
Small	20.000	30.303	24.657
Marginal	20.408	29.787	25.000
Landless	20.000	28.571	25.000
Total	**21.323**	**32.089**	**26.765**

Source: Field Survey.

Table 4.7

Total literacy by the size classes of the households and the regions

Size Category	*Kandi*	*Plain*	*Total*
Large	38.095	38.000	34.177
Medium	33.333	48.148	42.592
Small	23.529	31.884	27.272
Marginal	24.509	32.989	28.643
Landless	20.000	33.333	28.000
Total	**26.071**	**36.491**	**29.931**

Source: Field Survey.

Table 4.8

Sex ratio by the size classes of households and the regions

Size Category	*Kandi*	*Plain*	*Total*
Large	960.000	750.000	818.181
Medium	837.820	1000.000	914.062
Small	623.913	901.234	913.294
Marginal	836.206	906.542	869.955
Landless	750.00	882.352	827.586
Total	**868.589**	**892.226**	**882.539**

Source: Field Survey.

Table 4.9

Area owned per sampled Household (in acres) by the size classes of households and the regions

Size Category	*Kandi*	*Plain*	*Overall*
Large	8.142	6.8	7.352
Medium	5.162	3.414	4.568
Small	3.189	2.045	2.639
Marginal	1.375	0.887	1.134
Landless	–	–	–
Overall	**3.16**	**2.186**	**2.673**

Source: Field Survey.

Table 4.10

Land per capita by size classes of households and the regions

Size Category	*Kandi*	*Plain*	*Overall*
Large	0.166	0.073	0.052
Medium	0.046	0.027	0.018
Small	0.017	0.130	0.007
Marginal	0.006	0.004	0.002
Landless	–	–	–
Overall	**0.005**	**0.003**	**0.002**

Source: Field Survey.

Table 4.11

Consumption expenditure on total cereals (in Rs.) per households for a period of 30 days by the category of the households and the regions

Size Category	*Kandi*	*Plain*	*Overall*
Large	571.43	557.50	563.235
	(37.37)	(34.60)	(35.71)
	(28.181)	(22.48)	(23.89)
Medium	441.90	474.73	457.50
	(37.86)	(38.10)	(37.98)
	(28.38)	(28.21)	(28.30)
Small	385.00	430.80	407.02
	(38.35)	(39.68)	(39.01)
	(29.34)	(28.44)	(28.88)
Marginal	308.75	326.71	313.48
	(37.70)	(38.28)	(37.98)
	(27.98)	(27.67)	(27.82)
Landless	236.00	237.14	233.66
	(40.60)	(35.46)	(37.43)
	(29.98)	(25.41)	(27.13)
Overall	372.05	394.40	383.22
	(37.97)	(37.90)	(37.94)
	(28.29)	(27.01)	(27.62)

Source: Field Survey.

Note: Figures in parentheses represent percentage of the total food expenditure and total expenditure. First = percentage of the total food and second = percentage of the total expenditure.

Table 4.12

Consumption expenditure on total milk and milk products (in Rs.) per household for a period of 30 days by the size category of the households and the regions

Size Category	*Kandi*	*Plain*	*Overall*
Large	275.43	290.00	284.00
	(18.01)	(18.00)	(18.01)
	(12.62)	(11.69)	(12.05)
Medium	181.66	184.47	183.00
	(15.56)	(14.81)	(15.19)
	(11.66)	(10.96)	(11.32)
Small	151.48	173.8	162.21
	(15.09)	(16.01)	(15.55)
	(11.54)	(11.47)	(11.51)
Marginal	118.87	116.41	117.66
	(14.51)	(13.99)	(14.26)
	(10.77)	(10.11)	(10.44)
Landless	79.00	100.71	91.66
	(13.59)	(15.06)	(14.49)
	(10.03)	(10.79)	(10.51)
Overall	145.83	159.95	152.89
	(14.88)	(15.37)	(15.14)
	(11.09)	(10.95)	(11.02)

Source: Field Survey.

Note: Figures in parentheses represent percentage of the total food expenditure and total expenditure. First = percentage of the total food and second = percentage of the total expenditure.

Table 4.13

Consumption expenditure on Pulses (in Rs.) per households for a period of 30 days by the size category of the households and the regions

Size Category	*Kandi*	*Plain*	*Overall*
Large	228.57	189.00	205.29
	(14.95)	(11.73)	(13.01)
	(10.47)	(7.62)	(8.71)
Medium	146.43	144.21	145.37
	(12.54)	(11.57)	(12.06)
	(9.40)	(8.57)	(8.99)
Small	120.03	117.60	118.86
	(11.95)	(10.83)	(11.39)
	(9.15)	(7.76)	(8.43)
Marginal	95.57	98.41	96.97
	(11.67)	(11.83)	(11.75)
	(8.66)	(8.55)	(8.61)
Landless	72.00	83.86	78.92
	(12.38)	(12.54)	(12.48)
	(9.14)	(8.98)	(9.05)
Overall	120.99	119.95	120.47
	(12.35)	(11.52)	(11.93)
	(9.20)	(8.21)	(8.68)

Source: Field Survey.

Note: Figures in parentheses represent percentage of the total food expenditure and total expenditure. First = percentage of the total food and second = percentage of the total expenditure.

Table 4.14

Consumption expenditure on Edible Oil (in Rs.) per households for a period of 30 days by the size category of the households and the regions

Size Category	*Kandi*	*Plain*	*Overall*
Large	51.14	77.20	66.47
	(3.34)	(4.79)	(4.21)
	(2.34)	(3.11)	(2.81)
Medium	69.00	73.31	71.05
	(5.91)	(5.88)	(5.89)
	(4.43)	(4.35)	(4.39)
Small	49.66	55.12	52.29
	(4.94)	(5.07)	(5.01)
	(3.78)	(3.63)	(3.71)
Marginal	43.32	41.59	42.47
	(5.29)	(5.00)	(5.14)
	(3.92)	(3.61)	(3.77)
Landless	35.6	33.14	34.16
	(6.12)	(4.95)	(5.40)
	(4.52)	(3.55)	(3.91)
Overall	50.59	53.97	52.28
	(5.16)	(5.18)	(5.17)
	(4.84)	(3.69)	(3.76)

Source: Field Survey.

Note: Figures in parentheses represent percentage of the total food expenditure and total expenditure. First = percentage of the total food and second = percentage of the total expenditure.

Table 4.15

Consumption expenditure on Meat, Fish and Eggs (in Rs.) per households for a period of 30 days by the size category of the households and the regions

Size Category	*Kandi*	*Plain*	*Overall*
Large	71.43	55.00	61.76
	(4.67)	(3.41)	(3.91)
	(3.27)	(2.21)	(2.62)
Medium	28.57	44.73	36.25
	(2.45)	(3.59)	(3.01)
	(1.83)	(2.65)	(2.24)
Small	22.22	40.00	30.76
	(2.12)	(3.68)	(2.94)
	(1.69)	(2.64)	(2.18)
Marginal	27.50	25.64	26.58
	(3.35)	(3.08)	(3.22)
	(2.49)	(2.23)	(2.35)
Landless	20.00	35.71	29.16
	(3.44)	(5.34)	(4.61)
	(2.54)	(3.83)	(3.34)
Overall	29.00	36.50	32.75
	(2.95)	(3.50)	(3.24)
	(2.20)	(2.49)	(2.36)

Source: Field Survey.

Note: Figures in parentheses represent percentage of the total food expenditure and total expenditure. First = percentage of the total food and second = percentage of the total expenditure.

Table 4.16

Consumption expenditure on Vegetables (in Rs.) per households for a period of 30 days by the size category of the households & the regions

Size Category	*Kandi*	*Plain*	*Overall*
Large	80.00	88.20	84.82
	(5.23)	(5.47)	(5.37)
	(3.66)	(3.55)	(3.59)
Medium	73.24	76.63	74.85
	(6.27)	(6.15)	(6.21)
	(4.70)	(4.55)	(4.63)
Small	68.92	62.60	65.88
	(6.86)	(5.76)	(6.31)
	(5.25)	(4.13)	(4.68)
Marginal	51.62	63.84	57.66
	(6.30)	(7.68)	(6.98)
	(4.67)	(5.55)	(5.11)
Landless	39.00	45.71	42.91
	(6.71)	(6.83)	(6.78)
	(4.95)	(4.89)	(4.92)
Overall	62.19	67.13	64.66
	(6.34)	(6.45)	(6.40)
	(4.73)	(4.59)	(4.66)

Source: Field Survey.

Note: Figures in parentheses represent percentage of the total food expenditure and total expenditure. First = percentage of the total food and second = percentage of the total expenditure.

Table 4.17

Consumption expenditure on processed Food (in Rs.) per households for a period of 30 days by the size category of the households & the regions

Size Category	*Kandi*	*Plain*	*Overall*
Large	55.00	50.70	52.47
	(3.59)	(3.14)	(3.32)
	(2.51)	(2.04)	(2.22)
Medium	44.43	43.42	43.95
	(3.80)	(3.48)	(3.64)
	(2.85)	(2.58)	(2.71)
Small	31.48	37.20	34.23
	(3.13)	(3.42)	(3.28)
	(2.39)	(2.45)	(2.42)
Marginal	24.00	29.35	26.64
	(2.93)	(3.53)	(3.22)
	(2.17)	(2.55)	(2.36)
Landless	14.00	21.43	18.33
	(2.40)	(3.20)	(2.89)
	(1.77)	(2.29)	(2.10)
Overall	31.98	35.57	33.77
	(3.26)	(3.41)	(3.34)
	(2.43)	(2.43)	(2.43)

Source: Field Survey.

Note: Figures in parentheses represent percentage of the total food expenditure and total expenditure. First = percentage of the total food and second = percentage of the total expenditure.

Table 4.18

Consumption expenditure on Sugar (in Rs.) per households for a period of 30 days by the size category of the households & the regions

Size Category	*Kandi*	*Plain*	*Overall*
Large	50.28	78.80	67.06
	(3.29)	(4.89)	(4.25)
	(2.30)	(3.17)	(2.84)
Medium	40.38	57.95	48.72
	(3.46)	(4.65)	(4.04)
	(2.59)	(3.44)	(3.01)
Small	38.29	46.08	42.04
	(3.81)	(4.24)	(4.02)
	(2.91)	(3.04)	(2.98)
Marginal	36.50	37.64	37.06
	(4.45)	(4.52)	(4.49)
	(3.30)	(3.27)	(3.29)
Landless	25.60	26.57	26.16
	(4.40)	(3.97)	(4.13)
	(3.25)	(2.84)	(2.99)
Overall	38.22	46.95	42.58
	(3.90)	(4.51)	(4.21)
	(2.90)	(3.21)	(3.07)

Source: Field Survey.

Note: Figures in parentheses represent percentage of the total food expenditure and total expenditure. First = percentage of the total food and second = percentage of the total expenditure.

Tbale 4.19

Consumption expenditure on Salt (in Rs.) per households for a period of 30 days by the size category of the households & the regions

Size Category	*Kandi*	*Plain*	*Overall*
Large	7.86	12.7	10.70
	(0.51)	(0.78)	(0.67)
	(0.36)	(0.51)	(0.45)
Medium	6.45	9.31	7.82
	(0.55)	(0.74)	(0.65)
	(0.41)	(0.55)	(0.48)
Small	8.48	7.00	7.77
	(0.84)	(0.64)	(0.74)
	(0.64)	(0.46)	(0.55)
Marginal	7.45	6.58	7.02
	(0.90)	(0.79)	(0.85)
	(0.67)	(0.57)	(0.62)
Landless	5.00	6.57	5.91
	(0.86)	(0.98)	(0.93)
	(0.63)	(0.70)	(0.67)
Overall	7.43	7.82	7.62
	(0.75)	(0.75)	(0.75)
	(0.56)	(0.53)	(0.55)

Source: Field Survey.

Note: Figures in parentheses represent percentage of the total food expenditure and total expenditure. First = percentage of the total food and second = percentage of the total expenditure.

Tbale 4.20

Consumption expenditure on Spices (in Rs.) per households for a period of 30 days by the size category of the households & the regions

Size Category	*Kandi*	*Plain*	*Overall*
Large	32.71	51.5	43.76
	(2.14)	(3.19)	(2.77)
	(1.49)	(2.07)	(1.85)
Medium	26.19	38.00	31.80
	(2.24)	(3.05)	(2.64)
	(1.68)	(2.25)	(1.95)
Small	29.52	33.44	31.40
	(2.90)	(3.07)	(3.01)
	(2.24)	(2.20)	(2.22)
Marginal	38.57	26.23	32.48
	(4.71)	(3.15)	(3.93)
	(3.49)	(2.28)	(2.88)
Landless	25.00	21.42	22.91
	(4.30)	(3.20)	(3.62)
	(3.17)	(2.29)	(2.62)
Overall	33.67	32.46	33.06
	(3.43)	(3.12)	(3.27)
	(2.56)	(2.22)	(2.38)

Source: Field Survey.

Note: Figures in parentheses represent percentage of the total food expenditure and total expenditure. First = percentage of the total food and second = percentage of the total expenditure.

Table 4.21

Consumption expenditure on Beverages (in Rs.) per households for a period of 30 days by the size category of the households & the regions

Size Category	*Kandi*	*Plain*	*Overall*
Large	48.28	81.00	65.88
	(2.89)	(5.02)	(4.17)
	(2.02)	(3.26)	(2.79)
Medium	46.86	53.42	49.97
	(4.01)	(4.28)	(4.14)
	(3.00)	(3.17)	(3.09)
Small	56.07	42.08	49.34
	(5.58)	(3.87)	(4.73)
	(4.27)	(2.77)	(3.50)
Marginal	36.97	37.43	37.20
	(4.51)	(4.50)	(4.50)
	(3.35)	(3.25)	(3.30)
Landless	19.00	33.57	27.50
	(3.26)	(5.02)	(4.35)
	(2.41)	(3.59)	(3.15)
Overall	43.82	45.72	44.77
	(4.47)	(4.39)	(4.43)
	(3.33)	(3.13)	(3.22)

Source: Field Survey.

Note: Figures in parentheses represent percentage of the total food expenditure and total expenditure. First = percentage of the total food and second = percentage of the total expenditure.

Table 4.22

Consumption expenditure on Fruits (in Rs.) per households for a period of 30 days by the size category of the households & the regions

Size Category	*Kandi*	*Plain*	*Overall*
Large	60.71	79.50	71.76
	(3.97)	(4.93)	(4.55)
	(2.78)	(3.20)	(3.04)
Medium	62.00	45.52	54.17
	(5.31)	(3.65)	(4.49)
	(3.98)	(2.70)	(3.35)
Small	42.59	40.00	41.34
	(4.24)	(3.68)	(3.96)
	(3.24)	(2.64)	(2.93)
Marginal	29.72	30.12	29.92
	(3.62)	(3.62)	(3.92)
	(2.69)	(2.61)	(2.65)
Landless	11.00	22.86	17.91
	(1.89)	(3.41)	(2.83)
	(1.39)	(2.44)	(2.05)
Overall	41.21	39.95	40.58
	(4.20)	(3.83)	(4.01)
	(3.13)	(2.73)	(2.92)

Source: Field Survey.

Note: Figures in parentheses represent percentage of the total food expenditure and total expenditure. First = percentage of the total food and second = percentage of the total expenditure.

Table 4.23

Consumption expenditure on Intoxicants (in Rs.) per households for a period of 30 days by the size category of the households & the regions

Size Category	*Kandi*	*Plain*	*Overall*
Large	92.85	110.00	102.94
	(14.20)	(12.66)	(13.19)
	(4.25)	(4.43)	(4.37)
Medium	64.28	76.31	70.00
	(16.49)	(17.47)	(16.98)
	(4.12)	(4.53)	(4.33)
Small	40.7	72.00	55.77
	(13.21)	(16.79)	(15.23)
	(3.10)	(4.01)	(4.49)
Marginal	60.00	64.28	62.50
	(19.33)	(14.48)	(16.79)
	(4.98)	(4.10)	(4.49)
Landless	60.00	64.28	62.50
	(29.12)	(24.32)	(26.04)
	(7.62)	(6.89)	(7.16)
Overall	56.00	66.00	61.00
	(16.71)	(15.72)	(12.77)
	(4.25)	(4.52)	(4.39)

Source: Field Survey.

Note: Figures in parentheses represent percentage of the total food expenditure and total expenditure. First = percentage of the total non-food and second = percentage of the total expenditure.

Table 4.24

Expenditure on Fuel & Light (in Rs.) per households for a period of 30 days by the size category of the households & the regions

Size Category	*Kandi*	*Plain*	*Overall*
Large	55.00	70.50	64.12
	(8.41)	(8.11)	(8.21)
	(2.51)	(2.84)	(2.72)
Medium	45.47	50.78	48.00
	(11.66)	(11.62)	(11.64)
	(2.92)	(3.01)	(2.96)
Small	39.81	42.60	41.15
	(12.91)	(9.93)	(11.23)
	(3.03)	(2.81)	(2.92)
Marginal	28.37	30.00	29.17
	(9.97)	(9.41)	(9.69)
	(2.57)	(2.60)	(2.59)
Landless	27.00	27.14	27.08
	(13.10)	(10.27)	(11.28)
	(3.42)	(2.90)	(3.10)
Overall	36.85	40.95	38.90
	(11.00)	(9.75)	(8.14)
	(2.80)	(2.80)	(2.80)

Source: Field Survey.

Note: Figures in parentheses represent percentage of the total food expenditure and total expenditure. First = percentage of the total non-food and second = percentage of the total expenditure.

Table 4.25

Expenditure on Clothing (in Rs.) per households for a period of 30 days by the size category of the households & the regions

Size Category	*Kandi*	*Plain*	*Overall*
Large	205.00	313.00	268.53
	(31.35)	(36.04)	(34.42)
	(9.35)	(12.62)	(11.39)
Medium	121.66	149.73	135.00
	(31.21)	(34.28)	(32.75)
	(7.81)	(8.89)	(8.35)
Small	102.59	146.20	123.55
	(33.27)	(34.11)	(33.74)
	(7.57)	(9.65)	(8.76)
Marginal	83.62	92.69	88.10
	(29.39)	(29.08)	(29.23)
	(7.57)	(8.05)	(7.82)
Landless	51.00	80.71	68.33
	(24.75)	(30.54)	(28.47)
	(6.48)	(8.65)	(7.83)
Overall	103.60	138.10	120.85
	(30.93)	(32.89)	(25.31)
	(7.88)	(9.45)	(8.71)

Source: Field Survey.

Note: Figures in parentheses represent percentage of the total food expenditure and total expenditure. First = percentage of the total non-food and second = percentage of the total expenditure.

Table 4.26

Expenditure on Footwear (in Rs.) per households for a period of 30 days by the size category of the households and the regions

Size Category	*Kandi*	*Plain*	*Overall*
Large	61.43	101.50	85.00
	(9.39)	(11.68)	(10.89)
	(2.81)	(4.09)	(3.60)
Medium	34.14	52.58	42.90
	(8.75)	(12.03)	(10.41)
	(2.19)	(3.12)	(2.65)
Small	36.85	47.60	42.02
	(11.95)	(11.10)	(11.47)
	(2.80)	(3.14)	(2.98)
Marginal	26.12	34.36	30.18
	(9.18)	(10.78)	(10.01)
	(2.36)	(2.98)	(2.67)
Landless	21.00	32.14	27.50
	(10.19)	(12.16)	(11.45)
	(2.66)	(3.44)	(3.15)
Overall	32.82	48.69	40.80
	(9.82)	(11.59)	(8.54)
	(2.50)	(3.33)	(2.94)

Source: Field Survey.

Note: Figures in parentheses represent percentage of the total food expenditure and total expenditure. First = percentage of the total non-food and second = percentage of the total expenditure.

Table 4.27

Expenditure on Miscellaneous Goods and Services (in Rs.) per households for a period of 30 days by the size category of the households & the regions

Size Category	*Kandi*	*Plain*	*Overall*
Large	66.57	104.50	88.88
	(10.18)	(12.03)	(11.39)
	(3.05)	(4.21)	(3.78)
Medium	76.81	65.26	71.32
	(19.70)	(14.94)	(17.30)
	(4.93)	(3.87)	(4.41)
Small	50.40	74.20	61.84
	(16.34)	17.31)	(16.88)
	(3.84)	(4.89)	(4.38)
Marginal	55.87	45.00	50.50
	(19.64)	(14.11)	(16.75)
	(5.06)	(3.91)	(4.48)
Landless	26.00	40.71	34.58
	(12.62)	(15.40)	(14.40)
	(3.30)	(4.36)	(3.96)
Overall	58.05	61.80	59.92
	(17.32)	(14.72)	(12.55)
	(4.41)	(4.23)	(4.31)

Source: Field Survey.

Note: Figures in parentheses represent percentage of the total food expenditure and total expenditure. First = percentage of the total non-food and second = percentage of the total expenditure.

Table 4.28

Expenditure on Durable Goods (in Rs.) per households for a period of 30 days by the size category of the households & the regions.

Size Category	*Kandi*	*Plain*	*Overall*
Large	172.86	169.00	170.58
	(26.44)	(19.45)	(21.86)
	(7.19)	(6.81)	(7.23)
Medium	47.38	42.10	44.87
	(12.15)	(9.63)	(10.88)
	(3.04)	(2.50)	(2.77)
Small	37.96	46.00	41.82
	(12.31)	(10.73)	(11.42)
	(2.89)	(3.03)	(2.96)
Marginal	35.50	33.58	34.55
	(12.48)	(10.53)	(11.46)
	(3.21)	(2.92)	(3.06)
Landless	21.00	19.28	20.00
	(10.19)	(7.29)	(8.33)
	(2.66)	(2.06)	(2.29)
Overall	47.55	50.85	49.20
	(14.19)	(12.11)	(10.30)
	(3.61)	(3.48)	(3.54)

Source: Field Survey.

Note: Figures in parentheses represent percentage of the total food expenditure and total expenditure. First = percentage of the total non-food and second = percentage of the total expenditure.

Table 4.29

Expenditure on All Food Items (in Rs.) per households for a period of 30 days by the size category of the households and the regions

Size Category	*Kandi*	*Plain*	*Overall*
Large Farmer	1528.85	1611.10	1577.23
	(70.04)	(64.97)	(66.90)
Medium Farmer	1167.14	1245.73	1204.47
	(74.96)	(74.03)	(74.50)
Small Farmer	1003.78	1085.72	1043.17
	(76.49)	(71.69)	(74.08)
Marginal Farmer	818.75	831.61	825.16
	(74.21)	(72.29)	(73.24)
Agricultural Labour	581.20	668.71	632.25
	(73.83)	(71.67)	(72.50)
Overall	979.75	1040.37	1010.06
	(74.52)	(71.25)	(72.80)

Source: Field Survey.
Note: *Figures in parentheses represent percentage of the total expenditure.*

Table 4.30

Expenditure on All Non Food Items (in Rs.) per households for a period of 30 days by the size category of the households and the regions

Size Category	*Kandi*	*Plain*	*Overall*
Large	653.71	868.50	780.05
	(29.96)	(35.03)	(33.10)
Medium	389.76	436.78	412.21
	(25.04)	(25.97)	(25.50)
Small	308.37	428.60	366.17
	(23.51)	(28.31)	(25.92)
Marginal	284.50	318.71	301.39
	(25.79)	(27.71)	(26.76)
Landless	206.00	264.28	240.00
	(26.17)	(28.33)	(27.50)
Overall	334.97	419.79	377.38
	(25.48)	(28.75)	(27.20)

Source: Field Survey.
Note: Figures in parentheses represent percentage of the total consumption expenditure.

Table 4.31

Expenditure on Food and Non Food items (in Rs.) per households for a period of 30 days by the size category of the households and the regions

Size Category	*Kandi*	*Plain*	*Overall*
Large	2182.57	2479.60	2357.29
Medium	1556.90	1682.52	1616.57
Small	1312.15	1514.32	1409.34
Marginal	1103.35	1150.33	1126.55
Landless	787.20	933.00	872.00
Overall	1314.72	1460.00	1387.44

Source: Field Survey.

Table 4.32

Expenditure on Food and Non-food items (in Rs.) per person for a period of 30 days by the size classes of the households and the regions

Size Category	*Kandi*	*Plain*	*Overall*
Large	311.79	269.52	284.21
Medium	267.99	262.03	265.01
Small	199.03	245.83	220.74
Marginal	206.23	218.84	212.40
Landless	178.90	204.09	193.83
Overall	224.74	241.35	233.18

Source: Field Survey.

Table 4.33

Expenditure on Food and Non-food items (in Rs.) per consuming unit for a period of 30 days by the size classes of the households and the regions

Size Category	*Kandi*	*Plain*	*Overall*
Large	265.70	261.56	263.12
Medium	263.66	256.35	260.00
Small	184.61	242.67	210.65
Marginal	201.89	217.04	209.25
Agricultural Labour	195.82	193.79	194.55
Overall	214.79	237.07	225.96

Source: Field Survey.

Table 4.34

Incidence of poverty as per the Farm Business (FBI) criterion by the regions and total sampled population

Item	*Value*		
	Kandi	*Plain*	*Overall*
Head Count Ratio	62.22	49.42	55.71
Gini Co-efficient for Poor	0.31	0.34	0.33
Sen's Measure	45.98	40.13	43.05

Source: Field Survey.

Table 4.35

Incidence of poverty and Income Concentration as per Total Net Returns (TNR) criterion by the regions and total sampled population

Item	*Value*		
	Kandi	*Plain*	*Overall*
Head Count Ratio	42.90	27.60	35.12
Gini Co-efficient for Poor	0.210	00.16	0.180
Sen's Measure	22.73	12.47	17.23

Source: Field Survey.

Table 4.36

Incidence of poverty by per capita consumption expenditure for last 30 day's criterion and consumption inequalities by the regions

Item	*Value*		
	Kandi	*Plain*	*Overall*
Head Count Ratio	41.88	29.91	35.71
Sen's Measure	18.14	12.36	14.74

Source: Field Survey.

Table 4.37

Incidence of poverty by per consumer unit consumption expenditure for the last 30 day's criterion and consumption inequalities by the regions

Item	*Value*		
	Kandi	*Plain*	*Overall*
Head Count Ratio	41.57	27.89	35.82
Sen's Measure	19.17	11.71	15.70

Source: Field Survey.

Table 4.37(a)

Regions have been ranked in the descending order of magnitude

Item	*Kandi*	*Plain*
Educational Level of the Respondents	R^2	R^1
Male Literacy	R^2	R^1
Female Literacy	R^2	R^1
Total Literacy	R^2	R^1
Sex Ratio	R_1	R^2
Average Size of Household	R_1	R^2
Land Per Capita	R_1	R^2
Farm Business Income Per Capita	R^2	R^1
Net Returns Per Capita	R^2	R^1
Per Capita of Assets Owned	R^2	R
Per Capita Total Monthly Expenditure	R^2	R^1
Total Expenditure on Non-Food Items	R^2	R^1

Source: Field Survey.

Table 4.38

Size Classes Have Been Ranked in the Descending Order Using Following Indicators

Indicator	*Large*	*Medium*	*Small*	*Marginal*	*Landless*
Male Literacy	R^2	R^1	R^5	R^3	R^4
Female Literacy	R^1	R^2	R^5	R^3	R^3
Total Literacy	R^2	R^1	R^5	R^3	R^4
Sex Ratio	R^5	R^1	R^2	R^3	R^4
Average Size of Household	R^1	R^2	R^3	R^4	R^5
Land Per Capita	R^1	R^2	R^3	R^4	R^5
Farm Business Income Per Capita	R^1	R^3	R^2	R^4	R^5
Total Net Returns Per Capita	R^5	R^5	R^2	R^1	R^4
Assets Owned Per Households	R^1	R^2	R^3	R^4	R^5
Per Capita Monthly Total Consumption Expenditure	R^1	R^2	R^3	R^4	R^5
Non-Food Exp-enditure	R^1	R^2	R^3	R^4	R^5

Source: Field Survey.

5

Land Reforms, IRDP and Poverty

Agricultural economy of Jammu and Kashmir has undergone significant changes after Independence. There has been not merely quantitative increase in agricultural production and productivity but also qualitative improvements in terms of techniques and practices heralding the process of agricultural transformation. The strategy of agricultural transformation ahs envisaged the annihilation of 'Built-in-depressors' through a set of institutional and technological reforms.

A. Changes in the Institutional Infrastructure

The niggardliness of agriculture is sometimes attributed to a set of particular cultural values, which are related to work, thrift, industriousness and aspirations for a higher standard of living. This view suggests that poor agriculture is essentially a cultural characterization of the way people live. Many sociologists believe that farmers are ' hard headed' and regard traditional practices as providing security. Thus, for the present "innovation often seems to constitute a direct attack on his way of life or a complete break with it" (Doment, R. & Rosier, B. (1970). Prof. Gunnar Myrdal, the Nobal Laureate, has aptly pointed out that the farmers' behaviour patterns in underdeveloped countries are deeply rooted in attitudes hardened into more by along historical process. They have been given a foundation by institutions, particularly those of economic and social stratifications, in the first hand related to land ownership and tenure, that have been consequential in determining the use of land" (Myrdal, K.G. (1971). It is thus argued that change in the institutional framework of agriculture is a pre-requisite for the transformation of subsistence agriculture into a modern dynamic sector.

On the eve of Independence the institutional framework of agriculture in the Jammu and Kashmir state was dominated by the feudal or semi-feudal relations. The land tenure system had become more exploitative, oppressive and regressive and thus was considered responsible for the prevalence of poverty and misery in the rural areas. It was argued that emancipation of peasantry from the bondages of institutional depressors will unleash forces which will raise levels of productivity and production in agriculture.

With the view to eliminate the institutional depressors the State Government abolished Jagirs and Muafis in 1948 and the land thus available was thrown open to cultivation by tenants. By another act protected tenancy rights were conferred on tenants at will possessing 17 kanals (irrigated) or 33 kanals (un-irrigated) and in Kashmir and 33 kanals (irrigated) or 65 kanals (un-irrigated) in Jammu Province. However, it was with the Enactment of Big Landed Estates Abolition Act of 1950 that the real change in the institutional setting of the agrarian economy was sought. The main features of this legislature were [Report of Agriculture Census (1970-71)].

a. Fixation of a ceiling on the holding of proprietors at 22¾ (182 kanals) of land excluding orchards, fuel and fodder reserves and uncultivable waste land;

b. Expropriation of proprietors from areas exceeding the ceiling;

c. Transfer of tenanted areas from which owners were expropriated to tillers in cultivating possession thereof, without compensation;

d. Fixation of a ceiling at 160 kanals including land already held by them in ownership rights in respect of lands transferred to tillers in proprietorship;

e. Such lands from which proprietors were expropriated and were not in cultivating possession of any person, escheated to the state.

Due to this Act about nine thousand proprietors were expropriated from 4½ lakh acres of land held in excess of such a ceiling. Out of this 2.3 lakh acres were transferred in ownership right to the tillers free of any encumbrances while the remaining land wasted in the State. In the following years various amendments were made to the Tenancy Act and in 1965 all non-occupancy tenants were deemed to be protected tenants provided the land held by them did not exceed 2 acres of irrigated or 4 acres of un-irrigated in Kashmir and 4 acres of irrigated or 6 acres of un-irrigated land in Jammu province.

The Land Commission set up by the Government of Jammu and Kashmir in 1963 to examine the existing land laws emphasized the need to abolish landlordism, as it was not only a matter of social justice but also a necessary step towards raising the agricultural production and productivity.

Another Bill known as "The Jammu and Kashmir Agrarian Reforms Bill 1972" which had sought some bold and drastic changes in the agrarian setup was made non-operative in 1975 by the State Government. However, after suitable modifications in the Bill, Jammu and Kashmir Agrarian Reforms Act was passed in 1976 with the following features:

a. The Act envisaged the basic principle of land to the tiller.

b. The Act extinguishes with effect from 1st May, 1973 rights of all owners or intermediaries of land not cultivating it personally in Kharief 1971 provided that an ex-owner who wants to cultivate land personally will have the right to resume part of such land subject to certain conditions;

c. According to the class of soil and availability or otherwise of irrigation the ceiling area of 12½ standard acres varies from 9 acres to 25 ordinary acres. The Act provides that this ceiling area is related to a family consisting of a person, his or her spouse and their children excluding a married daughter and a major son, separated from his parents and holding land in his own name.

It was believed that the implementation of this Act will make available approximately four thousand acres of land as surplus for distribution among landless and land-poor persons and the tillers of about 5 lakh acres of land shall acquire ownership rights.

Owing to land reform measures the Government has succeeded in eliminating considerably the elements of exploitation from the agrarian system. It has abolished the Zamindari System, protected the tenancy rights, regulated the rents, and distributed the surplus land among the landless, marginal and sub-marginal tillers of the soil. These measures undoubtedly have strengthened peasant proprietorship in the State, which is considered by all standards, conductive to the speedy transformation of agriculture. The tenurial status of holdings as was obtained in 1970-71 is presented in Table 5.1.

It can be seen from the Table 5.1 that all types of tenurial holdings are concentrated in the size category of less than 2½ acres for instance, of the wholly owned and self operated category 74.80 percent of the holdings accounting for 34.28 percent of the area are in the size class of less than 2½ acres as against 14.80 percent holdings embracing 24.27 percent area in the size class of 2½ to 5 acres whereas in the size category of 25 acres and above there are only 677 wholly owned and self-operated holdings accounting for an area of 32333 acres. Similarly, of the partly owned and partly ranted holdings 63.93 percent accounting for 24.87 percent of the areas are in the size category of less than 2½ acres. The concentration of the holdings wholly rented from others in the size category of less than 2½ acres is also observed from the table. Thus, it can be concluded that not only the marginal and sub-marginal holdings still dominate the agricultural scene in the State but also that the parasitism in the agrarian structure of the State economy has yet not been eliminated completely.

In addition to the Land Reforms the State Government has also made consented efforts to extend the philosophy of cooperation to the different agricultural activities so as to create institutional framework capable of supporting a progressive and exploitation free agrarian system. It is indeed irony of fate that the efforts of the State to cooperatives the agricultural sector have not yielded the desired results on this front excepting a limited success in the promotion of cooperative credit societies.

These changes in the institutional setting of Jammu and Kashmir Agriculture have warranted increased flow of financial resources so as to promote production and productivity of this sector.

Size and Structure of Holdings

Despite these reforms the agrarian structure of Jammu and Kashmir economy continues to be dominated by marginal and sub-marginal holdings as can be observed from Table 5.2.

The information contained in Table 5.2 reveals that 31.04 percent holdings are in the size category of less then 5 kanals (5/8 acres) and account for only 5.64 percent of the area with an average size of holdings estimated at 0.42 acres. Another depressing aspect of the structure of holdings is that 63.83 percent of the holdings are in the size category of less than 2 acres and account for only 23.45 percent of the area with an average size of holdings estimated as 0.85 acres. A further look on the data provided in the table shows that

88.60 holdings are in the size category of less than 5 acres and account for only 56.73 percent of the area. In contrast to this, 8.80 percent of the total holdings in the size category of 5 acres to 10 acres account for 26.15 percent of the area while as 2.6 percent of the holdings in the size category of 10 acres and above account for 17.12 percent of the total area.

These observations lead to the inevitable conclusions that:

i. There is uneven distribution of area in the different size category of holdings;

ii. The magnitude of parameterization is very high in the state. If this phenomenon is viewed temporally it is observed that the percentage of holdings in the size category of 'below 5 acres' has been increasing from 73.34 percent in 1950 to 77.21 percent in 1960 and 88.6 percent in 1970.

Besides the size of operational holding in the State estimated at 2.31 acres is the lowest in the country excepting Kerala where it is estimated at 1.73 acres, as is reflected in Table 5.3.

The low size of operational holding in the State may be responsible for the niggardliness of agriculture. But it can also be argued that the disadvantage in size may be nullified by intensive cultivation as has been done in Japan where the average size of holding, estimated at 2.96 acres is also low.

Efforts to raise production and productivity in an agricultural setting dominated by marginal and small farmers essentially imply larger investments. It in turn suggests a still greater flow of funds to agriculture.

SECTION II

IRDP AND POVERTY

The target oriented direct attack on poverty was mounted in J&K during the Sixth Five Year Plan. Various nationally designed programmes were initiated to help bottom deciles of the rural population achieve incomes above the poverty line. This chapter examines the impact of these programmes on rural poverty in the state with special reference to Jammu region. The state governments claims of successes are critically discussed in the context of the evaluation studies of (a) the National Institute of Rural Development (NIRD), Hyderabad (1986); (b) "The Evaluation Study of IRDP" by the Directorate of Economics and Statistics, J&K Government (1988); (c) the report of J&K Bank Ltd. (1986).

This section of chapter has been further sub-divided into three sections. In sub-section I official claims about the performance of various poverty have been recapitulated briefly. Sub-section II presents a review of the various studies. The major conclusions have been summed up in the concluding section.

The IRDP - the key component of the anti-poverty programme - was launched in 75 "Approved Blocks" in 1981-82. Later, all the 113 blocks were covered under the programme to raise the income generating potential of various activities. The sector-wise activities identified for the purpose were:

a) **Agriculture**: Seeds, storage bins, agricultural implements, tarpaulin's, mushroom cultivation and feeding tubs;

b) **Horticulture**: Spray tubs/buckets, spray machines and implements ;

c) **Allied Activities**: Dairy units, sheep units and fisher units;

d) **Soil Conservation**: Area terracing, leveling etc.

The schemes were launched with the explicit purpose of helping small and marginal farmers, sharecroppers, agricultural labourers and rural artisans to cross the poverty line.

Allocation and Expenditure

The allocation and expenditure on the various components and schemes of the IRDP for the period 1980-81 to 1987-88 is presented in Table 5.4. The Sixth Plan provided for a total outlay of Rs. 4,500 crores for the implementation of IRDP. An investment of 35 lakh was earmarked for each block. However, the actual outlay and expenditure have been of the order of Rs. 41.34 crores and 28.96 crores respectively. The allocation and expenditure on various schemes exhibited an upward trend during the period (Table 5.1). However, the expenditure has lagged behind allocations at the district and divisional levels.

The official estimates claims resounding success of the various schemes undertaken under IRDP in the state. Thus, out of the 4,70,477 families below poverty line, approximately 3,07,541 families are claimed to have been raised above the poverty line during 1981-82 to 1988-89. It has also been claimed that the achievements have outstripped the targets in most of the districts..

IRDP in the Jammu District

The Integrated Rural Development Programme (IRDP) was first of all introduced in the Akhnoor block of the district during 1980-81. From 1981-82 onwards, it was introduced in all other blocks of the district. It is now being implemented in 9 blocks out of 11, of Jammu district (excluding Jammu district by District Rural Development Agency (DRDA) and in 2 blocks Vijaypur and Samba by Command Area Rural Development (CARD) Agency. DRDA is operating in 9 blocks but the central assistance has been made available for 8 recognized blocks only. No central assistance is available for the Satwari Block that was created a few years ago.

At the time of inception of IRDP in Akhnoor block, 1306 units were established under different schemes with a subsidy amount of Rs. 4.62 lakh. According to 1984-85 household survey conducted in the district 68,905 families were found to be living below poverty level, 23,497 families were assisted and a subsidy of Rs. 220.19 lakh was provided to them (DRDA). The year wise appraisal of the families assisted (Ref. Table 5.5) under IRDP indicates that during the period from 1980-81 to 1989-90, 37,257 families were assisted in Jammu district. Out of these, 10,007 were scheduled caste, 774 were women beneficiaries and 318 were given second dose of assistance. During Six Five Year Plan, 5,227 (14.16%) scheduled caste families received benefit under the programme. The table further reveals that except 1986-87, the percentage of scheduled caste beneficiaries' show an upward trend during Seventh Five-Year Plan. The percentage of women beneficiaries also increased from 0.92 per cent during 1985-86 to 16.72 per cent during 1989-90. The percentage of beneficiaries given the second dose of assistance was 2.10%, 4.14%, 4.80% and 3.76% during the period 1986-87, 1987-88, 1988-89 and 1989-90 respectively.

During Sixth Plan period bank loan amounting to Rs. 391.05 lakh was raised by the DRDA. In all, 23,497 beneficiaries were assisted against the target of 24,595 and subsidy amounting to Rs. 220.19 lakh was provided to them against the target of Rs. 300.80 lakh. The targets during the years 1980-81, 1982-83 and 1983-84 exceeded the targets *i.e.* 112 per cent, 101 per cent and 117 per cent respectively. Whereas, during the remaining two years it remained below the targeted numbers, *i.e.* 86.70 per cent and 79 per cent during 1981-82 and 1984-85 respectively (Singh, Jasbir).

The block wise performance of Integrated Rural Development Programme during Sixth Five Year Plan shows that the highest number of beneficiaries were assisted in Akhnoor block during the plan period followed by Parmandal Block (109 per cent achievements), Bhalwal Block (108 per cent achievements) and so on.

The block wise financial outlay and expenditure under IRDP for Jammu district during Sixth Five Year Plan period reveals that there was not a single block, which had fully, utilized the allocated outlays. It remained 82 per cent in

Parmandal, 81 per cent in Satwari, 75 per cent in Akhnoor, 73 per cent in Bhalwal, 72 per cent in R.S. Pura, 67 per cent in Marh, 58 per cent in Bishnah, 51 per cent in Dansal and 39 per cent in Khour.

Block wise data for the Seventh Five Year Plan is available for 1987-88 to 1989-1990; none of the nine blocks of Jammu district could achieve the physical targets. It further shows that in 92 per cent cases each in Marh and Bhalwal, 90 per cent in Akhnoor, 83 per cent in Bishnah, 79 per cent each in Dansal and R.S. Pura, 76 per cent in Parmandal, 71 per cent in Satwari and 69 per cent in Khour block physical targets were achieved.

The block wise available data shows that during 1988-89 and 1989-90 financial expenditure exceeded the outlay in Bhalwal (115 per cent) and in March block (106 per cent) whereas it was below outlay in the remaining blocks of the district (Singh Jasbir).

The government claims of successes/achievements have been critically examined by various organization/individuals. The various evaluation exercises give a radically different picture of the working and impact of the IRDP. In the following pages the main findings of various studies have been presented with a view to judge the validity of the official claims.

NATIONAL INSTITUTE OF RURAL DEVELOPMENT STUDY

A study conducted by the National Institute of Rural Development (NIRD), Hyderabad in 1986 to evaluate IRDP in two districts viz., Udhampur district in Jammu and Anantnag district in Kashmir revealed that—

a) in none of the blocks of the selected districts was the formulation of comprehensive block plans attempted. Lack of adequate and expert staff at the block level inhabited the preparation of such exercise;

b) the indifference of the top level executives at the state level resulted in failure to undertake a base line survey for the identification and selection of the beneficiaries and for the implementation of the schemes. The IRDP action plan, as such, was based on arbitrary assumptions leading to faulty formulation of schemes and failure at the implementation level;

c) the selection of beneficiaries was adhoc and the formulation of action plans were mere official formality. No genuine effort was made to prepare the scheme profiles to guide the beneficiaries and banks;

d) the official guidelines were flouted in a variety of ways. The state level coordination committee (SLC) fixed the norms only on the basis of the size of schemes; geophysical and economic conditions were ignored. The bankers, being solely motivated by target fulfilling considerations in advancing loans, ignored the income-generation aspects. The selection of beneficiaries was done without regard to the norms stipulated in the guidelines. The block officials and village panchayats were not involved in the decision making process. The selection was left to VLW's who could not be free from personnel predilections and biases;

e) nearly 33.3 per cent of the families (in both districts) selected were not below the poverty line. The rate of rejection of loan applications was above 20 per cent (average for all banks) and cases pending were above 34 per cent. In other words, a large section of the identified beneficiaries were denied loans. The banks accepted only 45 per cent applications;

f) villages located in far off places were not covered under the schemes. The material/assets purchased through the private suppliers (the earlier practice of procuring these from outside the state having been discarded earlier) provided to be inferior and costlier which escalated the unit costs;

g) the fake supply of assets and the circulation of the same assets among various beneficiaries was found to be a common practice. Corruption and misuse of funds was found to be a common. However, it was more pronounced in case of: dairy animals, bullocks, sheep and goat rearing schemes;

h) the monitoring of the schemes during pre and post implementation period was not very sound. The identity cum monitoring and Vikas Patra - basic instrument of monitoring was not distributed to the beneficiaries and the few that were distributed remained unutilized;

i) the unit costs varied from scheme to scheme ranging from Rs. 605 (tailoring under TRYSEM) to Rs. 11,855 (agricultural implements and mechanical threshers) in Udhampur district and Rs. 1,745 (ISR - Wicker Willow) to Rs. 5,875 (Sericulture) in Anantnag district;

j) the average net annual income for different schemes ranged between Rs. 123 for plough bullock/ supply scheme to Rs. 4,178 for retail karyana store in Udhampur district and Rs. 4,669 for willow wicker (cottage industry) in Ananatnag district. The net return from plough bullocks in Anantnag district was about 6 times more than that in Udhampur district due to higher levels of agricultural development in the former;

k) the output - input ratio for the schemes varied from 1.10 (plough bullock) to 3.41 (tailoring) in Udhampur district and 1.41 (dairy) to 2.21 (sericulture) in Anantnag district. Schemes like tailoring showed a high input output ratio, the net incremental income from them being much less to help the beneficiaries cross the poverty line. The schemes in the animal husbandry sector had low capital output ratio and the net incremental income was low.

THE 'EVALUATION STUDY OF IRDP' by the Directorate of Economics and Statistics, J&K Govt. (Code 002/1937/J&K January, 1988).

The Draft Report on the Evaluation Study of IRDP by the Directorate of Economics and Statistics, J&K Govt. (Code 002/1937/J&K) is very critical of the Govt. claims. The report points out that 'according to the annual plan documents issued from the Planning Department from year to year, the total number of families covered under income generating scheme is 2.35 lakhs for 1980-81 to 1986-87. Two Directors of Rural Development indicate a total of 2.40 lakhs families for 1981-82 to 1986-87. This makes an average of 0.40 lakhs per year for the period. But careful examination of the figures shows that the number is inflated by inclusion of sizeable chunk of families assisted with non-income generating schemes giving only paltry benefit of less than Rs. 200 per family by way of subsidy on items like seed bins, tarpaulin, agricultural implements etc. which do not make any addition to the family income. A total of 0.91 lakh families of this latter category are included. For removing this fallacy, we subtract the number of families with non-income generating assets schemes. In this way, the actual number covered under income generating schemes during 1981-82 to 1986-87 shrinks to 1.49 lakh only. Data collected from DRDA's and from the BDO's (which should be more realistic) put the actual achievements still lower at 1.25 lakhs.

The report further points out 'that about 21 per cent of identified families have been covered under income generating schemes. The field enquiry reveals a wastage/ leakage of about 27 per cent in the covered number, which would reduce net coverage of the total identified families to about 15 per cent only or 2.5 per cent per year. This is less than the growth rate of population of over 2.6 per cent for the state. But the growth rate among the identified families should be much higher as they make the poorest strata of society. Hence increase in the size of the backlog of the number of target groups.

Regarding targets and achievements under income generating schemes, the reports points out that 'the actual achievements have been to the extent of one third of targets in the beginning with the passage of time, however, the percentage of achievements has improved'. The percentage for 1986-87 is above 75 per cent. However, efforts are needed to reduce further the gap between targets and achievements.

On financing the IRDP, the report points out that 'assistance to the beneficiaries is in the shape of loan, subsidy and own resources . . . Thus, nearly 67 per cent of the finance came from loans and 33 per cent from subsidy. It appears no effort is made to mobilize the private resources. There is need to motivate the beneficiaries to mobilize the private resources in the trade and industries sectors at least' and that 'the average finance per unit works out as Rs. 4,200. This includes Rs. 2,009 as loan, Rs. 1,304 as subsidy and Rs. 7 only as own finance. The amount of average finance has been relating higher in the later years than in the earlier years'.

As far as TRYSEM is concerned the report points out that 'according to the information contained in the annual plan documents, a total 0.27 lakh youths has been trained under the TRYSEM programme from 1980-81to 1986-87 making an average of nearly 1000 per year ..... the data about disposal of the trained youths are incomplete and not very clear. However, the field data....., reveal that not more that 10 per cent of the trained youth have utilized their training. Further the total number of households assisted under the non income generating schemes is indicated as 0.83 lakhs in the two regions. Under these schemes price subsidy is given on purchase of various articles. Seed bins, tarpaulin, shalimar plough, cutters, carding equipment, cattle feed, tubs, spray pumps etc.

"A sample of 111 beneficiaries was taken for field enquiry. Average benefit of Rs. 177 by way of subsidy on agricultural implements, seed bins, tarpaulin etc. has accrued per beneficiary. However, out of 111, 19 or (17%) denied to have been beneficiaries, while 92 or 83% agreed to have got the benefits".

The report has the following to say on wastage. "The wastage of coverage occurs of following accounts as revealed by the sample study".

	Reasons	*Percentage*
(i)	Death of asset animals	1.01
(ii)	Units not existing	5.34
(iii)	Assets sold by beneficiary	4.80
(iv)	Beneficiary denied to have taken loan	2.00
(v)	Assets not obtained/got cash and not assets	2.86
(vi)	Beneficiary not located	3.56
(vii)	Cases under process	0.21
(viii)	Assets existing but defunct	1.08
	Total Wastage	**26.89**
(ix)	Units existing	73.11
	Total	**100.00**

"Thus, there is wastage of 27 perc ent. In addition over 17 per cent of the beneficiaries have been mis-selected as they were already above the poverty line" [page 48].

About the selection of target group families, the report points out that "the Destitutes account 35 percent, "very very poor" 52 percent, "very poor" 9 percent and the "poor" 4 per cent. the number said to be brought under income generating schemes ending 31st march, 1987 is 4381 which include 1604 or 37% "poorest of the poor", is 2295 (52%) "very very poor"

351 (8%) "Very poor" and 131 or 3% "poor". The poorest have to be tackled first. However, the selection made so far is almost in proportion to the total strength in each category" [page 20].

Further, "the income generating schemes have given income benefits to some of the beneficiaries. The concentration of the beneficiaries in the groups of "Restitutes" and "very very poor": has been reduced from 56 per cent to 18 per cent. But the shift has been mostly to the categories of "very poor" and "poor". Only 20 per cent have moved above the poverty line (17 per cent were already above this line) 63 per cent continue to live below this line in spite of having been covered under the programme" (page 48).

In the concluding observations the report says, "The database of the Rural Development Organization is very weak. Some of the data are not available at all. The data available suffer from gaps and in consistencies... A number of beneficiaries could not be located. A good number have denied taking the loans. Sizeable numbers of units were non-existent. Many have managed to obtain cash and misutilised it rather than taken the assets. These leakages in the programme need to be plugged... A good number of beneficiaries had not belonged to the target group, viz., below the poverty line as seen from their income estimates... A good number of beneficiaries have disposed off their assets because these were thought to be of poor quality and unprofitable. Many of the animals like milch cows, pack animals, sheep, draughts animals are reported to have died.... some units are defunct... A good number of beneficiaries have complained that loan was not given to them in full as sanctioned. Some feel that the amount of subsidy was not given to them in full... Non-income generating schemes do not add to the income of the beneficiaries and are not, therefore, a right charge on the IRDP... There appears to be no linkage between the selection of youth for training in various trades and the potential available (page 50-52).

THE REPORT OF THE J&K BANK LTD. 1986

The lead bank department of the J&K Bank Ltd. conducted a survey of the IRDP in Kupwara block of north Kashmir. In its report published in February, 1986, the bank pointed out that "IRDP is yet to take off properly and it has not so far benefitted the target groups to any great extent. On the basis of norms providing assistance to 600 families per block per annum for six recognized blocks, the year wise performance is reflected in the following Table:

Year	*No. of benifi-ciaries to be covered under IRDP*	*No. of benifi-ciaries provided assistanc*	*% coverage*
1979-80	3600	717	19.62
1980-81	3600	866	24.00
1981-82	3600	699	19.42
1992-93	3600	906	25.17
1983-84	3600	1357	37.69

"Due to low performance, the agency had to carry over unspent balance of Rs. 30.82 lakhs during 1983-84 and Rs. 4.30 lakhs as on 1st April , 1985 in respect of subsidy component reorientation and reorganization of DRDA is required" (page 15-16).

About the IRDP operational problems, the report says "most of the beneficiaries do not figure in the list". List of the poorest of the poor has not been prepared/finalized. However, beneficiaries are sponsored/selected on adhoc basis. There is a gap of one month to even three months in effecting procurement and disbursement of loans sponsoring of cases is not strictly in accordance to scheme wise and physical targets appearing in the annual action. Plans in respect of a particular bocks... Quality of sponsoring has been poor and selective out of 100 beneficiaries, one is a person of good land holdings and property, one is a govt. contractor and three govt./private employees. It has also been revealed that there is not pre-sanction visit conducted by financing banks and no regular follows up" [page 16].

The target oriented group approach has become the main strategy of poverty removal in India since 1980. Conflicting evidence has accumulated over the years about the rationale and operational efficacy of the various programme. Perfect targeting obviously is a pre-requisite for the success of the programme. However, it has been observed "perfect targeting of public expenditure to those below the poverty line is, of course, a policy makers pipe dream. In reality, the administrative costs of scheme which attempt even moderate targeting turn out to be excessive and any scheme which relies on bureaucratic vetting of low income households on a case by case basis is open to corruption and manipulation". (Kanbur, 1989). In practice, the policy maker has options that are somewhere between the two extremes of perfect targeting and no targeting at all. Usually the policy instrument available allow a distinction to be drawn between broad sub-groups in the population and expenditure can be directed towards these sub-groups and it being understood that there will be leakages to those above the poverty line within each sub-group. The hope is that by using the different income distribution characteristics of different groups, in particular, their different patterns of poverty, to guide the allocation rules for public expenditure, better targeting towards the poor can be achieved than by treating groups identically" (Kanbur, 1989).

The official view in India is that the strategy has paid off and a substantial fraction of the below poverty population has been pulled up. On the other hand many non-official studies have demonstrated that the strategy has not fulfilled the stated objectives and that it needs to be reformulated. It has been suggested that the strategy needs to be redesigned and supplemented with wage employment programme (Rath 1985). Some economists have advocated institutional/

structural changes and an acceleration in agricultural growth as the main instruments of poverty removal (Rao, 1988).

The radical view, "traces the problem to the absence of structural changes in society", and says that "unless society is radically restructured and productive assets are more equitably distributed, the poorer section of the population cannot benefit from the gains of development" (Samuel and Subramanium, 1983).

The micro and macro studies conducted to evaluate the programme, particularly the IRDP across the various parts of the country, have arrived at the broad conclusion that:

(a) a significant number of beneficiaries have been wrongly identified and that a good proportion of the households were not poor;

(b) the assets provided to the beneficiaries through purchase committees have been of inferior quality;

(c) mostly the beneficiaries have been provided livestock units and that only a small percentage of the beneficiaries are left with livestock assets after the grounding of the scheme;

(d) Supportive and marketing services and facilities are not paid adequate attention to sustain the programme on long term basis;

(e) the implementing agencies frequently indulge in corruption and other malpractices such as manipulation of loans/schemes;

(f) the mismatch between the various programmes/ schemes provided enough space to the officials to misuse funds;

(g) the number of beneficiaries who crossed poverty line does not exceed 40 per cent under the IRDP (IMFR, 1984; NABARD, 1984). Some other estimates show a lower rate of success (Ahuja, 1984).

The design and operation of anti-poverty programme in Jammu district has virtually followed the all India pattern. Except for appropriately aligning the various schemes under IRDP with the demands of the local environment, no significant difference is discernible in the execution of various schemes.

The official data and evaluation studies reveal that there has been a persistent gap between allocations and expenditures in the entire anti-poverty programme in J&K. The shortfalls in expenditure disprove the argument of 'resources crunch' in the state.

The State government claims a high rate of success in the implementation of IRDP. An official document of the state government reads, "As per the survey conducted in 1983, 4.76 lakh families were identified living below the poverty line. During the Seventh Five Year Plan, 3.43 lakh families were assisted with an investment of Rs. 27 crores. The balances of 1.26 lakh are expected to be covered during the next plan. The 38th round of NSS, which placed the number at 1.26 lakhs, did not corroborate the state govt. estimate of 4.76 lakhs families as below poverty line in 1983. Further more the official data about the number of households brought above the poverty line has been contested by various evaluation studies. The IRDP has been plagued by wrong identification, wrong selection of schemes and leakages.

According to NIRD study nearly 33.3 per cent selected families in the districts of Udhampur and Anantnag were not below the poverty line. The Directorate of Eco and state. J&K Government points out over 17 per cent of the beneficiaries has been mis-selected as they were already above poverty line. Bhatt and Talashi pointed out that 36 per cent households assisted were below poverty line. The J&K Bank Survey reports that not all the beneficiaries were really poor. All evaluation studies speak of delays in the sanctioning of loans, rejection of loan certificates, indifference of the top-level administration, failure to implement schemes properly, corruption and misutilisation of the funds as the chief causes of the partial failure of IRDP to fulfil the targets.

Table 5.1

Tenurial Status of Holdings

Tenurial Status	*Size Category*					*Total*
	Below	*2½ to 5*	*5 – 10*	*10 – 25*	*25 acres*	
1. Wholly-Owned & Self Operated:						
a. Number	410149	81161	44083	12290	677	548360
b. Area	412381	291890	300420	165884	32333	1202908
2. Partly owned-and ranted						
a. Number	129496	40558	24074	8051	381	202560
b. Area	153502	152289	177273	116273	17792	617129
3. wholly rented from others						
a. Number	173033	32777	18014	3807	115	227746
b. Area	161394	113234	114637	49851	5448	444564

Source: *Compiled from the Report of the Agriculture Census* (1970-71), Government of Jammu and Kashmir, Tables 3 (a) and 3 (b), pp. 124 – 127.

To conclude, it can be said that the anti poverty programme may not have fully succeeded in eradicating poverty but they have succeeded in raising the consciousness of the poor and that their poverty is systemic and congenital and that therefore, it can be overcome (Bhatt, M.S., 1994).

One can surmise that the administrative aspects have not received careful consideration at the decision making level. The administrative aspects, it has been argued consists of two components, implementation and strategy. The frequent transfer of official, inadequate assessment of the ability of beneficiaries to utilize programme service and carelessness in identifying the beneficiaries, not to speak of instances of corruption, have been identified as the cause of implementation failures [Paul and Subramina, 1983]. Even if the officials and bureaucracy are honest and dedicated, failures are caused by strategic reasons. A very significant field report has emphasized that careful attention to programme strategy might make a difference to the accrual of benefits to the weaker section (Madras Institute of Development Studies: structure and intervention: An evaluation of DPAD, IRDP and related programme in Ramanathapuram and Bharmapuri districts of Tamil Nadu, 1980).

Table 5.2

Size and Structure of Holdings

S.No	*Size Category*	*No of Holdings*	*Percentage*	*Area*	*Percentage*	*Average Size*
1.	Below 5/8 acres	303729	31.04	127673	5.64	0.42
2.	5/8 to 1¼ acres	179495	18.34	172311	7.61	0.96
3.	1¼ to 2 acres	141462	14.45	230940	10.20	1.63
4.	2 to 2½ acres	87992	8.99	196353	8.67	2.23
5.	2½ to 5 acres	154496	5.79	557413	24.61	3.61
6.	5 to 7½ acres	59977	6.13	365819	16.15	6.10
7.	7½ to 10 acres	26194	2.67	226511	10.00	8.65
8.	10 to 12½ acres	13584	1.39	151150	6.67	11.13
9.	12½ to 25 acres	10564	1.08	180858	7.99	17.12
10.	25 to 50 acres	1050	0.11	33940	1.50	32.32
11.	50 to 75 acres	67	0.01	3831	0.17	57.18
12.	75 to 100 acres	19	---	1653	0.07	87.00
13.	100 to 125 acres	9	---	982	0.05	109.11
14.	125 acres & above	28	---	15167	0.67	541.68
	Total	**978666**	**100**	**2264601**	**100**	**2.31**

Source: Report of the Agriculture Census (1970 - 71) Volume 1, Government of Jammu & Kashmir, pp. 176 – 177.

Table 5.3

Average Size of an Operational Holding

State	*Average (Acres)*
Rajasthan	13.49
Maharashtra	10.57
Gujarat	10.15
Madhya Pradesh	9.88
Haryana	9.34
Karnataka	7.90
Punjab	7.14
Andhra Pradesh	6.20
All India	5.68
Orissa	4.67
Himachal Pradesh	3.78
Bihar	3.75
Assam	3.63
Tamil Nadu	3.58
West Bengal	2.96
Uttar Pradesh	2.87
Jammu & Kashmir	2.32
Kerala	1.73

Source: Government of India, *All India Report on Agricultural Census*, 1970-71.

Table 5.4

Expenditure on IRDP in Jammu & Kashmir

Year	*Outlay*	*Expenditure*	*Expenditure as Percentage of Outlay*
6th Plan			
1980-83	N.A.	722.19	N.A.
1983-84	N.A.	652.19	N.A.
1984-85	904	393.00	43.47
Total 6th Plan	**2742**	**1767.38**	**64.45**
7th Plan			
1985-86	550.00	594.80	108.15
1986-87	620.00	666.50	106.53
1987-88	596.00	769.29	129.07
Total 7th Plan	**1766.00**	**2024.59**	**114.64**
Percentage of total 7th plan outlay spent in first three years	2300.00	2024.59	88.02

Source: Draft Annual Plans.
Note: Outlay includes matching amount assumed as central share.

Table 5.5

Number of families : Surveyed, identified, targeted and raised above poverty line in Jammu and Kashmir from 1981-82 to 1988-89

District	*No. of families surveyed*	*No. of families below poverty line*	*Beneficiaries covered*
Anantnag	61435	61435	56640 (92.19)
Baramulla	66068	52629	33887 (64.39)
Budgam	40242	36787	31112 (84.57)
Kupwara	37723	24424	16065 (65.78)
Pulwama	60266	32586	30753 (94.37)
Srinagar	31592	24003	14787 (61.60)
CAD	54763	21000	10553 (43.97)
Doda	8500	4600	17595 (73.31)
Jammu	77704	60000	34192 (56.99)
Kathua	22898	11000	6936 (63.05)
Poonch	26200	24000	9474 (22.56)
Rajouri	27538	24000	11598 (25.21)
Udhampur	56000	42000	21260 (101.24)
Kargil	10760	7000	8938 (127.69)
Leh	12613	3613	3751 (103.30)
	594302 **(80.09)Y**	**470477** **(79.16)X**	**307541** **(65.37)Z**

Note: Y = % of total rural household
X = % of families below poverty
T = In this case families have been covered under roaster dose. New targets were fixed in these district
Z = % of families below poverty line

Source: Directorate of Rural Development Jammu and Kashmir Division Govt. of J&K.

Table 5.6

Families Assisted under IRDP in Jammu District from 1980-81 to 1989-90

Year	No. of Benefi-ciaries	No. of SC Benefi-ciaries	% of SC Benefi-ciaries	No. of Women Benefi-ciaries	% of Women Benefi-ciaries	No. of Benefi-ciaries Covered under IInd Dose	%
1980-81	1306	120	9.19	-	-	-	-
1981-82	4682	739	15.78	-	-	-	-
1982-83	5463	971	17.77	-	-	-	-
1983-84	6320	1843	29.16	-	-	-	-
1984-85	5726	1604	2801	-	-	-	-
1985-86	5220	1708	32.72	48	0.92	-	-
1986-87	1762	16	.91	4	0.22	37	2.10
1987-88	2370	1053	44.43	124	5.23	98	4.14
1988-89	2680	1166	43.51	309	11.53	118	4.80
1989-90	1728	787	45.54	289	16.72	65	3.76
Total	**37257**	**10007**	**26.86**	**774**	**2.08**	**318**	**0.85**

Source: Complied from official records of Directorate of Rural Development, Jammu.

Table 5.7

Targets and Achievement under IRDP (Rs. in Lakh) in Jammu Distt. during Sixth Five Year Plan

Year	Physical		Financial		Bank Loan raised
	Target	Achievement	Outlay	Expenditure	
1980-81	1165	1306 (112)	3.80	4.62 (122)	11.05
1981-82	5400	4682 (86.72)	54.00	32.30 (60)	68.39
1982-83	5400	5463 (101)	69.00	41.87 (61)	81.46
1983-84	5400	3620 (117)	72.00	71.20 (99)	112.08
1984-85	7230	5726 (79)	102.00	70.20 (69)	118.07
Total	**24595**	**23497** **(96)**	**300.80**	**220.19** **(73)**	**391.05**

Source: Compiled from official records of District Rural Dvelopment Agency, Jammu.

Note: (i) Financial outlay includes subsidy only.

(ii) Figure in parenthesis shows percentage to total.

6

Conclusion and Summary

The phenomenon of poverty is not only colossal in its extent but also multi-faceted. The stark poverty is apparent and does not need the criteria and deeper analysis to recognize it. But the movement away from raw poverty and misery does pose the problems of identification of the poor and diagnosis and measurement of poverty. These problems of conceptualization and measurement of poverty have opened up a never ending debate for, poverty is too complex a phenomenon cutting across a myriad of economic, social, cultural, political and psychological factors. Therefore, controversies persist as how to define and measure poverty. The inter-regional and intra-regional variations in social and economic development, sparial land tenure systems, demographic structure, urbanization, wage structures, cultural modes, pattern and above all topography have not received adequate treatment in poverty studies. The failure at the conceptual and policy levels, to fully appreciate the regional dimensions of poverty has rendered the recommended poverty/nutritional norms suspect. Absence of attempts to identify poor households at regional and sub-regional levels (on the basis of rational socio-economic criteria) have left gates open to the non-poor families to take advantage of the anti-poverty programme. Region-specific studies on poverty have as such the potential of providing fresh analytical insights into the depth and magnitude of poverty problems for policy formulation.

Changes in the magnitude of poverty can be appreciated adequately if the impact of agrarian transformation and economic development on structural variables like income, consumption and assets are fully captured. The need for poverty studies at the sub-regional level assumes significance in view of the variation in attitude, climate and living conditions even within the same region.

In this background, the study of Incidence of Poverty Among Rural Scheduled Castes—A case study of Jammu Tehsil, assumes significance and thus was undertaken. The problem has been formulated and it has been determined in Chapter I. This chapter on the one hand, identified the main objectives of the present research work and on the other laid down a few hypotheses so as to concentrate on the some main aspects of the research problem. Further, analysis of Incidence of Poverty in India conclusively reveals the prevalence of poverty in varying degrees in the Pre British period. During the British period, it was not only deep but was deepening. In the post independence era, poverty alleviation automatically turned out to be one of the major objectives of the policies, aiming at socio-economic transformation of the country. Soon it was realized that growth by itself was not likely to reduce inequality and reduce poverty. This realization necessitated the comprehension and deeper analysis of poverty in its varied manifestations. Thus, investigations into the phenomenon of poverty centered around two inter-related themes, viz., inequality and poverty.

Chapter II entitled 'concept of poverty' starts with conceptual clarifications about the various concepts of poverty. An appendix to this chapter in which a synoptic view of the representative studies regarding the incidence of poverty in India spread-over the period 1948 to 1993 are given. The summary and conclusions of this chapter are as under.

Amongst different approaches opinions centering around the 'cultural traits of poor, biological inadequacies' and 'relative deprivation' constitute the core of widely discussed concepts of poverty. Oscar Lewis, one of the prominent protagonists of identifying the poor on the basis of their characteristics behaviour patterns and other attributes, defines 'culture of poverty' as a permanent way of life that develops among the poor people. Similarly, Rossi and Blum have identified the critical features of the poor. According to their view, culture of poverty is not only sustained by external environment but also by internal systems of values and preferences and inter-personal relationships that have a validity and life of their aim and that are capable of persisting well after the external circumstances have been modified or changed together 'Poverty' according to them "creates pathologies that block the ability to adopt at non-pathological situation". Since the culture of poverty concept highlights the negative traits of only the poor people and ignores the 'Culture of poverty' of the affluent who deliberately keep their fellow citizens poor therefore this view is less a culture of poverty, than the sociology of the underclass. The culture of poverty, concept defies measurement of a 'change', therefore social scientist attempted to define poverty in terms of a single quantifiable characteristic that all poor families and only poor families possess.

This necessitated the search for an objective definition of poverty with the attributes of measurability, objectivity, comparability and sensitivity to changes. Accordingly, in defining poverty emphasis shifted from cultural attributes of the poor to his biological needs in terms of minimum food requirements, biological conceptualization of poverty has two variants viz.,

(a) Subsistence criterion,

(b) Nutritional criterion.

According to subsistence criterion, poverty is a situation that denies minimum food and shelter necessary to maintain/ sustain life. The difficulty with this criterion is that the dividing line between the 'poor' and 'non-poor' is neither permanent nor uniform but changes both in space and time because it is conditioned by multiplicity of factors such as physical and climatic environment as well as the social structure and culture of the consuming unit. Besides, minimum requirements are also influenced by age, sex, vocation and other attributes of the consuming unit, which make standardization of a basket of necessities a difficult proposition.

Nutritional criterion associates poverty with the nutritional inadequacy and implies a minimum calorie in take below which there is under-nutrition along with some 'norm' for determining the minimum cost of an adequate diet. This criterion is also defective in as much as the quality and variety of food to be recommended to meet nutritional goals is dictated by the social conscience and customs of the consuming unit. There is also a dispute about using the average requirement based on the reference individual and equivalences for age and sex as the criterion to be used for judging the nutritional status of an entire population. Further, the criterion of nutritional adequacy in terms of minimum intake of calories per head per day as recommended by various organization and/or researchers lack agreement on the suggested minimum calories. These anomalies obviously are reflected in the estimated of Incidence of Poverty, and also in the policy measure to alleviate poverty.

The inequality approach to defining the poverty stresses that inadequality and poverty are congruent and hence co-terminus with each other. This approach emphasis's that inequality is concerned with the relative position of income groups to each other, hence poverty cannot be understood by isolating the poor and treating them as special group. It visualizes the society as consisted of a series of stratified income layers and stresses that poverty is connected with how the bottom layers fare relative to the rest of the society. It is while true that inequality and poverty are not unrelated to each other but they do not subsume each other. Reduction in income inequality may not, correspond to decline in poverty. Similarly, poverty may be intensified with the reduction in the level of income even when pattern of income distribution has remained unchanged. Further this approach ignores hunger and starvation, the two most important parameters of poverty.

Concept of poverty in terms of relative deprivation refers to conditions wherein people lack the basic elements to life and well being. Elaboration of this concept suggests that it is not possession of relatively less resources but only the incapacity to have the types of diets, participate in activities and enjoy living conditions and amenities that are customary in the society which would indicate that the people are in poverty. Besides the deprivation of resources, the concept also embraces the 'feeling' of deprivation connected with the want of opportunities to catch up with the better-privileged sections of the society. The concept is useful to understand poverty as a socio-economic and non-political phenomenon. However, it forms the weak basis of conceptualization of poverty for absolute deprivation constitutes the central idea of poverty.

Operative or policy definition of poverty reflects a balancing of community's capabilities and desires. Determination of an appropriate relationship between policy and polity is a difficult task for, it is influenced by multiplicity of factors including economic and non-economic and therefore may reflect objectives other than only the eradication of poverty. It must be remembered that inescapable poverty is still poverty.

Analysis of various approaches to defining poverty clearly reveals that the notion of poverty contains both absolute and relative dimensions, static and dynamic aspects and stocks and flow elements. The Biological and inequality approaches contain all these dimensions; aspects and elements, despite many infirmities, with suitable refinements constitute the basis of the most of the studies aiming at measurement and eradication of poverty.

Analysis of Incidence of Poverty in India conclusively reveals the prevalence of poverty in varying degrees in the Pre-British period. During the British period, it was not only deep but was deepening. In the post independence era, poverty alleviation automatically turned out to be one of the major objectives of the policies arming at the socio-economic transformation of the country. Soon it was realized that growth by itself was not likely to reduce inequality and reduce poverty. This realization necessitated comprehension and deeper analysis of poverty in its varied manifestations. Thus, investigations into the phenomenon of poverty centered around two inter-related themes, viz., inequality and poverty.

One of the earliest attempts to know the nature of income inequality is associated with the report of the committee on "Distribution of Income and levels of Living", setup by the Government of India in 1960 under the chairmanship of Prof. P.C. Mahalonobis. The committee submitted its report in 1964, but thereafter no similar effort was made to probe into this issue in-depth. Reserve Bank of India, National Council of Applied Economic Research and some individual researches notably Ojha and Bhatt (1963-64 & 1964-65), Ranadive (1961-62), Madalgi (1971), Dandekar and Rath (1960-61 to 1967-68), Tendulkar (1953-54 to 1975-76), Iyenagar and Brahamananda (1950-51 to 1983-84) have examined the pattern of income distribution at different points of time with the help of data, from different sources. All these studies suggest that during the period under review, income inequalities in the country were quite pronounced. The broad conclusions of these studies are:

a) Inequality is more pronounced in the pattern of income distribution than in the distribution of consumer expenditure.

b) Degree of inequality in income as well as expenditure is higher in urban than in the rural areas of the country; and

c) Inequality in the distribution of income and expenditure in both the rural and urban sectors has declined at current prices while at constant prices no firm trend is evident.

Along with the analysis of the pattern of income and expenditure distribution various estimates have also been made of the poverty line and proportion of people subsisting below it. One of the earliest studies is by a study group of the Planning Commission of India, it estimated Rs. 20 per month of 1960-61 prices as the bare minimum level of living, with no allowance for any expenditure on health and education. Several other estimates broadly confirm this. In his various studies Bardhan (1974) uses Rs. 15 for rural and Rs. 18 for urban areas to delineate poverty line while Dandekar and Rath (1971) suggest the same figure for rural but a higher figure of Rs. 22.5 for urban areas (all at 1960-61 prices). On the basis of these estimates Bardhan has suggested that in 1968-69 as many as 54 percent of the rural population were below the poverty line along with 41 percent of the urban population. Dandekar and Rath have reversed rural/urban populations, finding the relatively greater incidence of poverty to be in urban areas with 48.64 percent of the population below the level of poverty as against 33.12 percent in the rural areas. Ojha draws the line of demarcation between poor and non-poor at Rs. 18 per month in the rural areas and Rs. 11 in the urban areas and estimates that in 1960-61, approximately 51.8 percent of rural population as 184.2 million people and 7.6 percent or 6 million people in urban areas lived in poverty. Minhas adopts the figure of Rs. 240 per person per annum as a poverty line for the urban areas and Rs. 200 for rural population and arrives at the conclusion that people below the poverty line of Rs. 200 decreased from 173 million in 1956-57 to 154 million in 1967-68, that is, from 52.4 percent to 37.1 percent of the rural population. Vaidyanathan takes an income level of Rs. 132 per annum to denote poverty and finds that 15.7 percent of rural population in 1960-61 were living in poverty. Bhatty uses Sen's measure of poverty and head count ratio to estimate the Incidence of Poverty was most severe among agricultural labourers and the least among cultivators. Ahluwalia estimates the degree of poverty in rural India by using head count ratio and Sen's poverty index and concludes that the poverty line of Rs. 15 per capita per month, incidence of poverty increased to 57.9 percent of rural population in 1967-68 and thereafter declined to 47.6 percent in 1973-74.

Planning Commission, Government of India defined for the first time the parameters of poverty and spelt out the methodology in the technical note of the Sixth Five Year Plan. It adopted the physical survival definition and identified poverty line as the mid point of a monthly per capita expenditure of a class having daily calorie intake of 2,435 calorie per person in rural areas and 2,095 calorie per person in the urban areas which worked to Rs. 76 for rural areas and Rs. 88 for urban areas at 1979-80 prices and found that 48.4 percent of the country's population, 50.7 percent of the rural population and 40.3 percent of the urban population were living below the poverty line. In 1984-85, 37 percent of total population, 40 percent and 27.7 percent of rural and urban population respectively were living below the poverty level. The Seventh Five Year Plan demarcates the poverty line around Rs. 6,400 per annum per household or about Rs. 107 per capita per month at 1984-85 prices and estimate that population below the poverty line will come down to 25.8 per cent by 1989-90 while as it will be around 28.2 percent and 19.2 per cent in rural and urban areas respectively. Planning Commission optimistic projections envisage the proportion of population to fall below the poverty line to 10 per cent by 1994-95 and 5 per cent in the year 2000 A.D. estimates of the Planning Commission have come under scathing criticism of Raj Krishna, Vasant Gumaste, Sunderam and Tendulkar who have found deflects in the Planning Commission calculations of poverty line, crosses 57 million people during the first two years of Sixth Five Year Plan (1980-81 - 1981-82) and have worked out this figure at about 77 million people. Accordingly, their estimates reveal that the percentage of population below the poverty line in 1983-84 ranges between 46.5 to 48.8 percent and not 41.5 percent as suggested by the Planning Commission.

These studies on the delineation of the poverty line and the calculation of population below it have different reference dates, which account for variation in the estimates. Further, the minimum calorie intake is variously defined, usually between 2,100 to 2,400 per day. The composition of the diet incorporating the minimum nutritional requirements similarly varies and in a country of the geographic size and ethnic complexity of India, any single diet can only be an approximation. The prices used in costing the diet and the expenditure distribution into which the poverty line is projected are similarly liable to variation. For these reasons no single figure can be adopted with certainly and precision. Another criticism of the methodology is based on Sukhatme's argument that the recommended nutritional requirement (of say 2,200 or 2,400 calories) is recommended average and not a minimum which in itself suggests that in a population which is normally distributed with respect to height, weight, activity etc., half the people will have a calorie requirement below this recommended average. It is not only by comparing the distribution of requirements against the distribution of intake that can find the actual number of undernourished persons. A further source of inaccuracy in the conventional methodology for estimating the poverty line relates to the practice of blowing up the estimated cost of the necessary diet by a fixed ratio between food and non-food expenditure as obtained from consumption surveys. This pre-supposes that the recorded levels of food and non-food expenditure fall short of their basic minimum standards in the same proportion. The direction of the bias of this, however, cannot be easily established but its existence cannot be denied. Yet another source of error in the estimates of the proportion population in poverty, lies is the failure of the capture inter-family inequalities. Even families' members above the poverty line may include members who are seriously undernourished women; female child and old people most often come into this category.

Thus, poverty line like any other composite index, inspite of its usefulness in indicating the general magnitude of poverty cannot claim to be an accurate and precise measuring rod. It is therefore, important that its methodology be standardized and operational significance enhanced through continuous research.

Chapter III entitled "Planning Poverty Removal: The Indian Perspective" seeks to put the poverty problem in its national perspective against the existing literature on the subject. The main conclusions of this chapter are as under:

The poverty debate in India is an on going process. The persistence of object is not finally a game of numbers but impinges on vital issues relating to the structure of the economy and the nature of public interventions. The experiences of many countries show that initially anti-poverty programmes may have a trickle up rather than a trickle down (Adelman and Robinson). Conflicting evidence about the efficacy of anti-poverty programmes has accumulated in the country: while some studies have highlighted the success aspects, others have demonstrated the failure of the package to meet the objectives.

The twin objective of growth and social justice are complementary and an exclusive emphasis on either is likely to generate contradictions and pressures. While only sustained growth can ensure the eradication of poverty in the long run, the incidence of abysmal poverty and degradation in the immediate situation calls for public intervention. However, even the Planning Commission has acknowledged the limitations of the direct anti-poverty programmes.

It is imperative that the national policy should aim at ensuring a high rate of economic growth on a sustained basis. Large-scale anti-poverty programmes are likely to reduce the current growth rate. It has been estimated that at the current rate of growth of India would need a rate of growth around 12 -14 percent per annum to be able to eradicate poverty within next two decades (Gupta, 1989). Such a high rate of growth is un-attainable in the near future. As such a direct attack on poverty was perceived to be necessary. However, the trade-off between growth and anti-poverty programmes in terms of public outlays occur basically because: most antipoverty programme are transitory redistributive schemes and do not lead to the creation of permanent income generating assets for the poor (Krishan, 1990). Only sustained economic growth and sound public policies can ensure that the entitlement of poor are raised; otherwise there is a possibility that those who are pulled above the poverty line may slide back.

The important ingredient in any anti-poverty programme/strategy is targeting. While efficient selection of beneficiaries would reduce costs, the tendency to include even non-poor, tantamount to denying the genuinely poor the benefits of the programmes. While a certain amount of waste is inevitable due to the informational constraints yet there is ample scope to rectify these distortions.

Incidence of poverty has rarely been worked out along with income, assets and consumption inequalities. Changes in the levels of poverty cannot be appreciated adequately unless these are linked to the impact of agrarian transformation and economic development on structural variables like income, consumption and assets. The need for poverty studies at the regional or sub-regional level is self-explanatory. Such studies assumes significance in view of variation in attitude, climate and living conditions and as such provide fresh analytical insights into the dynamics of poverty. Against this backdrop the chapter seeks to explore the link between poverty and backwardness.

The incidence of poverty has been calculated with the help of Head Count Ratio and Sen's (1976) index. Further, we have made use of following criteria's.

i) Per capita per month monthly total consumption expenditure;

ii) Per consuming unit per month monthly total consumption expenditure;

iii) Farm Business Income (FBI distribution);

iv) Total Net Returns (TNR distribution).

The results are presented in chapter - IV.

The incidence of poverty according to above calculation indicates that incidence of poverty in the Kandi region is more than the Plain region. This confirms the view that more developed regions, low poverty ratio. The main conclusions of this chapter are:

i) Large farmers record the highest size of family and very low sex ratio while the converse is true in case of agricultural labourers.

ii) Among the regions the Plain region record higher sex ratio than the Kandi region.

iii) Size of ownership holding does not necessarily determine the level of education.

iv) The average size of the holdings works out to be highest in the Kandi region.

v) The pressure on land is more acute in the Plain region as compared to other regions. The region is agriculturally more developed.

vi) Marginal holdings turn out to be labour intensive. marginal farmers spend more on fertilizers, manure bullock labour.

vii) Land is the most important asset across the size classes and regions (except agriculture labourers). It constitutes more than 70% of the total assets help. Along with building the percentage goes as high as 90% of the assets.

viii) The Plain region is more developed region among

the regions and large farmers are the most prosperous among the size classes.

ix) Among the food items, cereals account for the major share of expenditure across the regions and size classes/categories.

The Plain region among the regions and large farmers from the size categories record the highest expenditure on the non-food items. The Plain region and the large farmers record the highest total expenditure per sampled households.

x) In the per capita consumption expenditure of the size classes, agricultural labourers and marginal farmers are lagging behind the large farmers.

xi) All poverty ratios' confirm the inference deduced from the ranking of regions according to difficult indicators. The more developed a region, lower the incidence of poverty.

The design and operation of the anti-poverty programmes in Jammu and Kashmir including the Jammu Tehsil has virtually followed the All India pattern. Except for appropriately aligning various schemes under IRDP with the demands of the local environment, no significant difference in the execution of various schemes. The official data and evaluation studies reveal that there has been a persistent gap between allocation and expenditure. The shortfall in expenditure disapproves the argument of 'resource crunch' so often used to explain the poverty in the state.

The state government claims a high rate of success in the implementation of IRDP and other poverty alleviation programmes. An official document of the state government reads, "As per a survey conducted in 1983, 4.76 lakh families were identified living below the poverty line as defined under the centrally sponsored scheme of IRDP. During the Seventh Plan period, 3.43 lakh families were assisted with an investment of Rs. 27 crores. The balances of 1.23 lakh families are expected to be covered during the Eight Plan period" (1990). The state government estimate of 4.76 lakh families as below the poverty line in 1983 was not corroborated by the 38th round of NSS which placed the number at 1.26 Lakh families. The official data about the number of households brought above the poverty line has been contested by various evaluation studies. IRDP programme has been plagued by wrong identification, wrong selection of schemes and leakages. According to NIRD study nearly 33.3 percent selected families in the districts of Udhampur and Anantnag were not below poverty line. The Directorate of Economics and Statistics, J&K Government points out over 17 percent of the beneficiaries have been mis-selected as they were already above poverty line. Similarly, Jasbir Singh's study points out 35.83% of selected beneficiaries were above the poverty line and net percent of beneficiaries crossing poverty line of Rs. 6,400 per family was just 32.50 percent because of IRDP.

All evaluation studies speak of delays in the sanctioning of loans, rejection of loan certificate, indifference of top level administration, failure to implement schemes properly, corruption and misutilisation of the funds as the chief causes of the partial failure of integrated rural development programmes to fulfill the targets.

One can surmise that the administrative aspects have not received careful consideration at the decision making level. The administrative aspects, it has been argued consists of two aspects, implementation and strategy. The frequent transfer of official, inadequate assessment of the ability of beneficiaries to utilize programme service and carelessness in identifying the beneficiaries, not to speak of instances of corruption, have been identified as the cause of implementation failure. Even if the officials and bureaucy are honest and dedicated, failures are caused by strategic reasons. A very significant field report has emphasized that careful attention to programme strategy might make a difference to the accrual of benefits to the weaker section. It can be said that the anti-poverty programmes may not have fully succeeded in eradicating poverty but they have succeeded in raising the consciousness of the poor and that their poverty is systemic and congenital and therefore it can be overcome. This also upholds our hypotheses that IRDP have made a positive contribution in decreasing poverty.

The agrarian reforms of early fifties provided the initial thrust to the modernization. Abolition of feudal institutions marked the first phase (1948) of the reforms measurement 4,000 acres of land were transferred to the tillers. In the second phase tenants on holding not exceeding 2.5 acres of wet land and 4.5 acres of dry land in Kashmir valley and almost double this size in respect of both categories in Jammu division. However, the third phase of the reforms (1950), which was decisive, abolished absentee landlordism completely. A ceiling of 22.5 acres was imposed on land ownership and surplus land was transferred to the tillers without compensation to the proprietors. Approximately, 2.3 lakh acres of cultivable land was transferred to 2 lakh tillers by the end of 1953 and about 8-lakh acres upto 1961. The 1950 Act specifically defined a cultivator as one who tilled the land with his own hand. To remove the flows and gaps the Agrarian Reform Act 1976 was promulgated. According to the provisional estimates of 1970-71 agricultural censuses, 29% peasants were expected to benefit from: 1976 Act. About 2.36 lakh families were covered under land reforms during 1981-82. Ownership rights have been extinguished for an area of 0.60 lakh hectares during 1981-82. Area on which absolute ownership rights have been conferred on the prospective owners is estimated at 0.10 lakh hectares during 1981-82 against 0.04 lakh hectares during the previous year. The basic tenets and objectives of 1976 Act are concerned these definitely marked, tangible improvement overall the previous acts. But the data about achievement under the act is not adequate to allow any serious evaluation. The implementation of the act has not been carried out with the sense of urgency and commitment, which the state witnessed during the fifties. From the analysis of land distribution it is obvious that compared to rest of the country, land distribution is less skewed in Jammu & Kashmir. This could be attributed to agrarian reforms undertaken in the state right from fifties (Bhat, M.S., 1994).

The state's experience in land distribution highlights the significance of land reforms in reducing asset inequalities in the rural areas where land occupies a key position in the asset structure. The analysis also shows a high degree of proliferations of marginal and tiny holdings. Studies have shown that given technology and cropping pattern, net returns from these holdings are low and most of these holdings are non-viable (Nissar, 1985; Sadhu, 89). This is a disturbing phenomenon of far reaching consequences. Changes in the techniques of production and cropping pattern can go a long way in making these holdings viable.

1. Income Transfer Through PDS

Though the PDS has mainly served the urban population in the past, in recent years its coverage of rural population has matched the urban coverage. The modest income support it provides in normal agriculture years must have marginally reduced poverty. However PDS benefits are not targeted to the poor as no means test is applied to determine the recipients. As a consequence, for a rupee spent, what the poor gets is much less than what they could have obtained with a better targeting scheme.

Not all the poor are able or willing to buy all of their ration entitlements at the going prices. As a consequence on a per capita basis the rich get a larger income subsidy than the poor. Many poor buy provisions for a day or two because of the lack of liquidity to buy, weeks ration at one time and in the process are forced to forgo bulk of their ration.

The direction in which PDS should be improved is obvious:

a) Coverage should be expanded in rural areas to cover as many poor as possible.

b) Better targeting to the poor is desirable. It should exclude the top 50 percent of the population, to begin with problems of identification and implementation do exist but a social climate may be created in which the well to do may be shamed into compliance.

c) One possibility of targeting would be to sell ration provision only for a day or two at a time. This would make it possible for the poor with cash shortage to avail of their ration entitlements to a greater extent. It will also discourage the well to do from buying rations because of the higher transaction cost.

2. Food Price Policy

The low output price and subsidized input price policy does help the poor. However, the burden of increasing subsidies for fertilizer water and electricity now strains the government budget to the point their continuation has become untenable low input prices lead to other distortions. When the marginal cost of water is nearly zero, a better water intensive cropping pattern gets selected and water is over used which may lead to water logging and salination problem. Low price of electricity for pumping water encourages over exploitation of ground water and discourages maintenance of pumps and conservation of energy. Similarly low fertilizer price also affects cropping pattern and leads to overuse of fertilizer.

The present policy of low food prices through input subsidy has now become untenable. It would be better to subsidize investment and support agricultural research rather than subsidizing current incurs - if cheap food is desired. Stepped up investment in irrigation can also be targeted to backward areas or to poorer farmers and therefore also has the potential to further alleviate poverty. Expansion of irrigation also generates additional employment. To make investment in irrigation in new areas more effective, research is also needed to adopt high yielding varieties to local-climatic conditions. Thus, low food prices realized through stepped up targeted irrigation and agricultural research would alleviate poverty more than input price subsidies.

3. Restoration of Common Property Resources

A major factor in worsening the quality of life of the landless and marginal farmers is the wide spread degradation and reduction due to encroachment of common poverty resources.

Loss of trees have deprived them of fuel wood, for which they now have to walk longer and spend more time gathering twigs etc., overgrazing has destroyed village pastures and the ability of the landless poor to keep their animals gainfully is reduced. Similarly, reductions in the capacities of village ponds and tanks have meant that the poor have less fish and water. Even the efforts at reforestation based on inappropriate trees have resulted in loss of artisan raw materials for the poor.

Thus, policies for the restoration of village commons can play an important role in poverty alleviation and in designing an approach to such policies. We should first understand why common property resources have come to the sorry state they are in and turned into waste land. A major factor is over harvesting of common property resources. But this has happened also because such resources are often government owned and the users have a right of use through convention. They did not perceive it as their own resource nor did they feel responsible for preserving its quality and sustained productivity.

What is needed is to provide each village exclusive right of use to a given piece of common property and to institute open democratic management of it. The strategy suggested for this by Aggarwal and Narain (1989) is the most promising of the various suggested schemes. They recommend a gram sabha (village assembly) equipped with appropriate laws and funds and supported by information, education, training, technical assistance and incentive schemes to manage such common properties. Decisions on the management have to be taken in the open gram sabha to ensure relevance and equity. (1, 2& 3 cited in Rural Poverty in India; Incidence, Issues and Policies; Dev Mahendra, Kirti Parikh & Suryanarayana, 1991)

4. Education and Skill Formation

Education takes time to be an effective anti-poverty policy. There is bit of a chicken and egg problem here. The poor can't afford to send their children to schools even when schools are free. The children are needed for productive work such as gathering fuel, do household chores, lookafter young siblings so that the mother can work.

The sad fact is that even today not all primary school going age children in India go to schools. Indian policy makers have not appreciated enough the role of literacy to spend the resources and efforts needed to ensure 100 percent attendance. Nor has schooling have been made compulsory. The allocation of resources by the government also suggests a relative neglect of primary education.

What is needed is to allocate much more resources for primary education, including provision of incentives to ensure that the children of the poor attend schools. Otherwise the problem of poverty will persist for years to come.

The poor are generally susceptible to ill health. Provision of safe drinking water and sanitation improvement in Primary Health Centres (PHC's) and immunization schemes seen to be the priority areas for improving the health to be poor. The primary health care system has achieved an impressive physical presence in a relatively short period. However, the quality of services is poor in many areas (World Bank, 1989). As a result, even many poor people under use these facilities.

It indicates that attention needs to be paid to strengthen the performance and quality of PHC services.

5. Agricultural growth in the region/state has been satisfactory. However, the cropping pattern is predominantly cereal-oriented. The possibilities of extending the margin of cultivation are almost negligible at the existing level of technology. Accelerated growth in agricultural production (both crop and non-crop) is central to poverty removal. Local specific techniques of production and land use are, in turn, crucial to this process. Under the present techniques of production, yields are low. The proliferation of marginal and small holdings. Parcelization of the holdings have further aggravated the problem. Diversification and intensification of agricultural operations should be accorded more attention. It is, therefore suggested that:

i) A comprehensive land survey using scientific methods.

ii) Extensive research to evolve farm technologies, suitable for each agro-climatic sub-region, so that small and marginal holdings become viable.

iii) Institutional, infrastructural and marketing support services for the full realization of the potentialities of the allied farm activities and non-crop sectors such as livestock, fishery, pisciculture and apiculture etc.

iv) The proliferation of the marginal and small holdings should be arrested. Similarly, parcelization of holdings needs to be reversed. This calls for a fresh look into the land policy consolidation of holding needs to be undertaken without further delay.

v) Cooperative marketing institutions need to be strengthened to avoid distress sales by small and marginal orchard's and poor artisans.

Land has to be treated as a binding constraint in the state. Micro-regions in the state should be taken as units of agro-climatic planning on a continuous basis so that resources can be utilized for income generation and poverty removal.

6. One of the core areas in the rural sector, which has lagged behind in the development, is 'Kandi' area. Its backwardness is, by and large, the peculiar constraints like poor accessibility, drought and lack of irrigation, poor soil and excessive soil erosion resulting in various ecological problems. In the sub-tropical region is the Kandi belt of Jammu spread over the entire Shiwalik Hills. The Jammu, Kandi are marked by poor vegetation cover, steep slopes and erratic rainfall resulting in serious drought-like conditions, the yields are low and due to poor returns, the people of the area, by and large poor. There is no institutional frame, which would help to build the necessary infrastructure for increasing the productive capacity of the area. The situation continues to be worse due to absence of any major industrial activity in the formal and informal sectors. The state government has formulated some special programmes in order to tackle the problems of Kandi areas - "Kandi Watershed Development Project" formulated by the Department of Soil Conservation. A recent study of Sadhu, A.N., has shown very encouraging results. It is hoped Kandi watershed programme is extended to other areas, so as they also reap the benefits of the programmes.

7. Attempts have to be made to redefine and refine the poverty line in context of the regions. The nutritional norms devised at the national level to determine the cut off poverty line assumes it is relevent across the space. This is hardly sustainable in view of the sharp variations in the food habits and consumption levels within and between the different micro regions in the state. Consumption surveys be conducted on regular basis in the micro regions to construct region specific poverty line and consumer price indices obviously an institutional agency consisting of geographers, nutrition experts, medical experts, economists and statistician has to be entrusted this multi-disciplinary work.

The anti-poverty programmes need to be streamlined

so that the benefits reach the genuine target groups. The first precondition is that the programmes should be partially released from the bureaucratic control. The identification of the scheme/beneficiaries, methods of targeting, implementation, evaluation, monitoring and resources allocation need to be recast keeping in view the requirements of each scheme. Innovative methods are called for in the executions of various anti-poverty schemes so that people readily adopt these schemes. The credit and delivery systems need particular attention. At the end of the day, it is the poor who will judge the relevance and efficacy of the anti-poverty programmes. The setting up of institutionalized agencies, which guarantee people participation in decision-making process, can ensure the success of the anti-poverty interventionist policy.

But if the poor are to benefit from these opportunities, they must have the awareness, self-assurance and the skills. Education plays a vital role in this.

Bibliography

Adelman & Robinson (1978), *Income Distribution Policy in Developing Countries—A case study of Korea*, Oxford University Press.

Ahluwalia, M.S. (1976), "Inequality, Poverty and Development," *Journal of Development Economics,* Vol. 3, No. 4.

Ahluwalia, M.S. (1978), "Rural Poverty and Agricultural Performance in India," *Journal of Development Studies*, Vol 14, No.3.

Aluwalia, M.S., et al. (1979), "Growth and Poverty in Developing Countries", *Journal of Development Economics,* Vol 6, No. 3.

Alagh, Y.K. (1991), "Indian Development Planning and Policy—An Alternative View," Wider Studies in Development Economics, Vikas Publishing House, New Delhi.

Atkinson, A.B. (1975), *The Economics of Inequality*, Oxford University Press, London.

Bandyopadhyay, D. (1988), "Poverty intervention Programmes For Poverty Alleviation", *Economic and Political Weekly*, Vol. XXIII, No. 26, June.

Bardhan, P.K. (1970), "On the Minimum Levels of Living and the Rural Poor", *Indian Economic Review*, Vol. V, No. 1, pp. 129-136.

Bardhan, P.K. and Srinivasan, T.N. (1971), "Income

Distribution Pattern Trends and Policies, Economic and Policies", *Economic & Political Weekly*, April 24.

Bhagwati, J. (1985), "Growth and Poverty", Lecture Delivered at Centre for Advanced Study of International Development, Distinguished Speakar, Series at Michigan State University.

Bhagwati, J.N. (1988), "Poverty and Public Policy", *World Development*, Vol. 16, No. 5, pp. 539-555.

Bhat, M.L. (1963), "Land Reforms in Jammu and Kashmir: A Review", *AICC Economic Review,* Vol. XV, No. 3, July 1.

Bhat, M.S. (1989), "A profile of Agrarian Scene in Jammu and Kashmir", in (ed.) M.L. Sharma et al., *Land Reforms in India, Achievements, Problems and Prospects*, pp. 89-111.

Bhat, M.S. (1990), "Agrarian Transition in Jammu and Kashmir—Achievements and Challenges", *Science and People*, Vol. 1, No. 2, March.

Bhat, M.S. (1990), "Poverty Alleviation Requires More Attention", in Georage Mathew, *Panchayati Raj in Jammu and Kashmir*, Institute of Social Sciences, New Delhi.

Bhattacharya, N., (1992), "Some observation on the Data Base for Poverty Studies", In Kadekodi, G K and G V S N Murthy (eds) *Poverty in India—Database Issues*, Vikas Publishing House, New Delhi.

Bardhan, P.K. (1974), "On the Incidence of Poverty in the Rural India in the Sixties", in Srinivasan, T.N. and Bardhan P.K., *Poverty and Income Distribution in India*, Statistical Society, Calcutta.

Bardhan, P.K. (1974), "The Pattern of Income Distribution in India: An Overviews", in Srinivasan, T.N. and Bardhan, P.K., *Poverty and Income Distribution in India*, Statistical Society, Calcutta.

Bardhan, P.K. (1984), "Land, Labour and Rural Poverty," *Essay in Development Economics*, Oxford University Press, New Delhi.

Bardhan, P.K. (1986), "Poverty and Trickle Down in Rural India: A Quantitative Analysis", in Dharam Narain (ed.), *Agricultural change and Rural Poverty, Variations on A Theme*, J W Mellor and G M Desai.

Brahmanada, P.R. and Panchmukhi, V.R.C (1987), *The Development Process of the Indian Economy*, Himalaya Publishing House, Delhi.

Bhattacharya, N. et al. (1991), *Poverty, Inequality and Prices in Rural India*, Sage Publications, New Delhi.

Bhattacharya, N. et al. (1991), "How do Poor Survive", *Economic and Political Weekly*, February 16.

Bhattachaurya, S.S. et al. (1980), "Regional Consumer Price Indices Based on Household expenditure Data", *Sarvekshana*, April.

Bhatty, I.Z., (1974), "Inequality and Poverty in Rural India", in Srinivasan, T.N., Bardhan, P.K., *Poverty and Income Distribution in India*, Statistical Publishing Society, Calcutta.

Borooah, V.K. (1992), "Problems in the Measurement of Inequality and Poverty: A Survey", *The Indian Economic Journal*, Vol. 38, No. 4.

Census of India (1981), *Jammu and Kashmir*, District Census of Jammu Districts.

Chakrabarti, S.K. et al. (1981), "Measurement of Incidence of Under nutrition", *EPW*, Vol. XVI, pp. 1275-78, August 1st.

Chakravarty, S. (1988), *Development Planning—The Indian Experience*, Oxford University Press, Delhi.

Chatterjee, A. (1990), "Household Consumer Expenditure Data of the Natioinal Sample Survey: An Appraisal", In

Tarlok Singh (ed.), *Social Science Research*, Concept Publishing House, New Delhi.

Chatterjee, G.S. and Bhattacharya, N. (1974), "On Disparities in Per Capita Household Consumption in India", In Srinivasan, T.N. and Bardhan P.K. (eds.), *Poverty and income Distribution in India*, Statistical Publishing Society, Calcutta.

Chatterjee, G.S. & Bhattacharya, N. (1975), "Some Observations on NSS Household Budget Data", In Dandekar, V.M. and Venkatarmia (eds.), *Database of Indian Economy: The Role of Sample Surveys*, Vol. II.

Choudhary, U.D.R. et al. (1981), "Poverty: Measurement and Concept", in Tarlok Singh (ed.) *Social Sciences Research and Problem of Poverty*, Concept Publishing House, New Delhi.

Coulter, B.P. (1989), "*Measuring Inequality—A Methodological Hand Book*", Westview Press, London.

Dandekar, V.M. (1980), "On the Measurement of Poverty", *Economic and Political Weekly*, Vol. XVI, No. 30, July 25.

Dandekar, V.M. (1982), "On the Measurement of Undernutrition", *Economic and Political Weekly*, Vol. XVII, No.6, Februray 6.

Dandekar, V.M. and Rath, N. (1971), *Poverty in India*, Indian School of Political Economy Poona.

Dantwala, M.L. (1973), *Poverty in India—Then and Now 1870-1970*, The Macmillan Co. of India Limited, Delhi.

Dantwala, M.L. (1985), "Garibi Hatao, Strategy and Options," *Economic and Political weekly*, Vol. XX, No 11, March 16.

De-Coasta, E P W (1971), "A Portrait of Indian Poverty" in *Challenge of Poverty in India*, ed., Vikas Publications, Delhi.

Dev, S.M. et al. (1991), "*Rural Poverty in India Incidence,*

Issues and Policies" Discussion Paper No. 55, Indira Gandhi Institute of Development Research.

Dhar, M.K. et al. (1987), "Land Use Pattern in Hill Agriculture: A Kashmir Study", *Agriculture Situation in India*, pp 165-168, June.

Edmudson, W.C. and Sukhatme, P.V. (1990), "Food and Work: Poverty and hunger", *Economic Development and Cultural Change*, The University of Chicago.

Fonseca, A. (1971), "The Poverty, Line for Industrial Workers", In Fonseca, AI, (ed.), *Challenge of Poverty of India*, Vikas Publications, Delhi.

Gaiha, R. (1987), "Poverty, Agricultural Growth and Prices in Rural India: A Critique and Extension", *Development and Change*, Sage Publications, London, Vol. 15, No. 4, 1987.

Gaiha, R. (1988), "On Measuring Risk of Poverty in Rural India" in Bardhan, P K and T N Srinivasan (eds.), *Rural Poverty in South-East Asia*, Oxford.

Gaiha, R. (1989), "Poverty, Agricultural Production and Prices in Rural India: A Reformulation", *Cambridge Journal of Economics*, Vol. 13, No.2, pp. 307-332.

Ghose, A. (1986), "On Reducing Poverty Speedily", *Yojana*, December, 16-31.

Gopalan, C. (1983), "Measurement of Undernutrition—Biological Consideration", *Economic and Political Weekly*, April 9.

Government of India (1969-90), *Fourth, Fifth, Sixth and Seventh Five Year Plans*, 1969, 1974, 1980-85, 1985-90.

Government of India, (1978), "Mannual on IRDP", Ministry of Rural Development, Delhi.

Government of India (1986), *IRDP and Allied Programmes—A Mannual*", Department of Rural Development, Ministry of Agriculture, New Delhi.

Government of Jammu and Kashmir (1968), "Report of the Land Commission", Ministry of Revenue, March.

Government of Jammu & Kashmir (1968), "Land Utilization Statistics", Directorate of Economics and Statistics.

Government of Jammu & Kashmir (1988), "Draft Report on the Evaluation Study of Intergrated Rural Development Programme", Diretorate of Economics and Statistics.

Government of Jammu and Kashmir (1970-85) "Report of Agricultural Censuses of 1970-71, 1976-77, 1980-81 and 1985-86."

Gupta, S.P. et al. (1983), "Measurement of Poverty—A Development Index", In *Regional Dimensions of India's Economic Development.*

Gupta S.P. (1986), *Poverty in India's Economic Development Strategies 1951-2000 AD*, (Ed.), J N Mongia, Allied Publisher Pvt. Limited, pp. 495-516.

Gupta, S.P. and Datta, K.L., (1984), "Poverty Calculation in the Sixth Plan", *Economic and Political Weekly*, Vol. XIX, No. 15.

Hicks, J. (1971), "Elimination of Poverty in India", in Fonseca, A I, (ed.), *Challenge of Poverty in India*, Vikas Publications, Delhi.

Hirway, Indira (1985), "Garibi Matao: Can IRDP Do It", *Economic and Political Weekly*, Vol. 20, No. 13, March 30.

Hirway, Indira (1988), "Reshaping IRDP", *Economic and Political Weekly*, Vol. XXIII, No. 26, June. 25.

Iyengar, N.S., (1983) "On Poverty Indicators", in *Regional Dimensions of India's Economic Development.*

Jain, L.R. et al. (1988), "Dimensions of Rural Poverty: An Inter-regional Profile.", *Economic and Political Weekly*, Special Number, November.

Jain, L.R. and Tendulkar, S.D. (1989), "Inter-temporal and Inter-Fractile - Group Movements in Real Levels of Living for Rural and Urban population of India: 1970-71 to 1983", *Journal of Indian School of Political Economy*, Vol. 1, No. 2, July - Dec. 99.

Jasbir, K. et al. (1985), "Socio-Economic Impact of IRDP in Punjab," *Kurukshetra*, August.

Jha, R. (1986), "What Ails IRDP", *Yojana,* Vol. 30, No. 16, September 1-15.

Jodha, N.S. (1988), "Poverty Debate in India : A Minority View", *Economic and Political Weekly*, Special Number, November.

Kakwani, N. (1980), "On a Class of Poverty Measures" *Econometrica*, Vol. 48, No.2, pp 437-446, March.

Kakwani, N. and Rao, S.K. (1990), "Rural Poverty and its Alleviation in India", *Economic and Political Weekly*, March 31.

Kaul, P.N. (1975), "Land Reforms in Jammu and Kashmir", *Indian Journal of Economics*, Vol. XXXVII, No. 147, April.

Khan, B.A. (1981), *Economic Consequences of Land Reforms in Jammu and Kashmir State*, University of Kashmir, (PhD. Thesis Unpublished).

Khusro, A.M. (1988), "Poverty of Poverty Analysis", *Development Perspective*, IEG, Delhi.

Krishanaji, N. (1981), "On Measuring Incidence of Undernutrition—A Note on Sukhatme's Procedure", *Economic and Political Weekly*, Vol. XVI, No. 22.

Krishna, R. (1980), "Income, Poverty and Unemployment", *Economic Times*, May 15.

Kurien, C.T. (1978), *Poverty Planning and Social Transformation*, Allied Publishers, New Delhi.

Kurien, C.T. (1992), *Growth and Justice*, Oxford.

Lakdawala, D.T. (1978), "Growth, Unemployment and Poverty", *The Indian Journal of Labour Economics*, Vol. 21, No. 1 and 2, April - July.

Lanjow, P. and Stren, N. (1991), "Poverty in Palanpur". *The World Bank Economic Review,* Vol. 5, No.1, pp. 23-55.

Madalgi, S.S. (1971), "Poverty in India—A Comment", *Economic and Political Weekly*, February.

Madalgi, S.S. (1968), "Hunger in Rural India 1960-61 to 1964-65", *Economic and Political Weekly*, Annual Number, January.

Malcolm, S.A. (1983), "The Triple Action Alone Can Remove Poverty", *Yojana*, Vol. 27, No. 3, February.

Mehta, B.C. (1990), "Measurement of Poverty", *Margin*, April-June.

Mehta, B.C. and Jain, Kusum (1989), *Assets, Liabilities and Rural Poverty*, Vol. 13, No. 2, July.

Mellor, J.W. and Desai, G.M. (1986), "Agricultural Change and Rural Poverty—Variations on a Theme," Oxford University Press.

Minhas, B.S. (1970), "Rural Poverty Land Redistribution and Development Strategy: Facts and Policy", *The Indian Economic Review*, Vol. V (New Series), April.

Minhas, B.S. (1990), "Rural Cost of Living et al., 1970-71 to 1983: States and All India", *The Indian Economic Review*, Vol. XXV, No. 1, pp. 75-104, January - June .

Manhas, B. S. et al. (1991), "Declining Incidence of Poverty in 1980's: Evidence Versus Artifacts", *Economic and Political Weekly*, Vol. XXVI, Nos. 27, 28, pp. 1673-1682, July 6-13.

Moynihan, Daniel P., *On Understanding Poverty*, Basic Books, Inc. Publishers.

Murthy, G.V.S.N. (1992), "Poverty: Measurement and Data Base Issues", In Kadekodi, G.K. and G.V.S.N. Murthy (eds), *Poverty in India—Database Issues*, Vikas Publishing House, New Delhi.

Myrdal, Gunnar (1968), *Asian Drama, An Inquiry into the Poverty of Nations*, 20th Century Fund, Pantheon Books, New York.

Nair, K.N. et al. (1990), "Structural Changes in Land Holdings in India", IDAAD Occassional Papers and Reprints, August.

National Institute of Rural Development Hyderabad (1986), *An Evaluation of IRDP in Udhampur and Anantnag Districts of J&K.*

Ojha, P.D. and Bhat, V.V. (1963), "Pattern of Income Distribution in India, 1953-54 to 1956-57", *Reserve Bank of India Bulletin*, Vol. 17.

Ojha, P.D. (1970), "A Configuration of Indian Poverty: In Equality and Levels of Living", *Reserve Bank of India Bulletin,* January.

Parikh, K. and Subramaniam (1992), "Data Needs for Poverty Alleviation Studies in Kadekodi, G.K. and G.V.S.N. Murthy (eds), *Poverty in India - Database Issues,* Vikas Publishing House, New Delhi.

Planning Commission, Government of India, *Evaluation Report on IRDP*, May.

Punit, A.E. (1982), *Profile of Poverty in India*, B R Publishing Corporation, Delhi.

Rao, V.K.R.V. (1981), "Measurement of Poverty", *Economic and Political Weekly*, pp. 1433-36, Aug. 29.

Rao, V.K.R.V. (1982), *Food Nutrition and Poverty in India*, Vikas Publishing House, Delhi.

Rath, N. (1985), "Garibi Hatao: Can IRDP Do It?", *Economic and Political Weekly*, February 9.

Rath, N. (1989), "Poverty, Alleviation and Employment", *Economic Times*, Mid Week Appraisal, July 6.

Rountree, B.S. (1922), *Poverty—A Study of Town Life*, Macmillan London.

Sadhu, A.N. and Singh, A. (1980), *New Agricultural Strategy: Its Implications*, Marwah Publications.

Sagar, S. (1988), *Poverty Measurement Some Issues*, RBSA Publishers, SMS Highway, Jaipur.

Saith, A. (1990), "Development Strategies and the Rural Poor", *The Journal of Peasant Studies*, Vol. 17, No. 2, pp. 171-244, Jan.

Sarma, P.P. (1987), *Dimensions of Rural Poverty*, Daya Publishing House, Delhi.

Sastry, S.A.R. (1980), "A Survey of Literature on Poverty, Income Distribution and Development", *Artha Vijnana*, Vol. 22, No.1, pp. 62-88, March.

Sawant, S. (1990), "Incidence of Poverty in Rural India", In Tarlok Singh (eds), *Social Science Research and Problem of Poverty*, Concept Publishing House, New Delhi.

Sen A .K. (1973), *On Economic Inequality*, Oxford University Press.

Sen, A K. (1974), "Poverty, Inequality and Unemployment: Some Conceptual Issues in Measurement", In Srinivasan, T.N. and P.K. Bardhan, *Poverty and Income Disribution in India,* Statistical Publishing Society, Calcutta.

Sen, A.K. (1976) , "Poverty: An Ordinal Approach to Measurement", *Econometrica*, Vol. 44, No. 2, March.

Sen, A.K. (1979), "Issues in the Measurement of Poverty", *Scand Journal of Economics*, 81, pp.285-307.

Sen, A.K. (1989), *Poverty and Famines - An Essay on Entitlement and Deprivation*, Claredon Press, Oxford.

Sen, A.K. (1979), "Issues in the Measurement of Poverty", *Scand Journal of Economics*, 81, pp. 285-307.

Sen, A.K. (1982), *Poverty and Famines: An Essay on*

Entitlement and Deprivation, Oxford University Press, New Delhi.

Shah, N.C. (1988), "Measurement of Poverty : An Interstate Profile", *Anvesak*, Vol. 18, Nos. 1 and II, June-December.

Sharma, A., *Concept and Measurement of Poverty*, Anmol Publications, New Delhi.

Sharma, J.N. et al. (1989), "Poverty, Measurement and Alleviation: A Survey of Literature", *REJ*, Vol. 13, No. 2, July.

Singh, J.S. (1996), *Working of Integrated Rural Development Programme*, Anmol Publications, New Delhi.

Singh, K. (1985), "IRDP: Some Policy and Management Issues", *Kurukshetra*, August.

Singh, M.L. (1986), "IRDP - Its Relevance for Future", *Indian Journal of Agricultural Economics*, Vol. 41, No. 4.

Sinha, S.K. (1976), "Land Reforms and Emerging Agrarian Structure in Bihar", *IJAE*, Vol. 31, No. 3.

Singhal, S. (1990), "Methodological Issues in Identifying the Poor", in Tarlok Singh (ed.), *Social Science Research and Problem of Poverty*, Concept Publishing House, New Delhi.

Srinivasan, T.N. (1974), "Poverty: Some Measurement Problems", *Conference Proceedings of the 41st Session of International Statistical Institute*, New Delhi.

Sukhatme, P.V. (1965), *Feeding India's Millions*, Asia Publishing House, Bombay.

Sukhatme, P.V. (1977), "Nutrition and Poverty", *Lal Bahudur Sharstri Memorial Lecture*, Indian Agricultural Research Institute, New Delhi.

Sukhatme, P.V. (1981). "On Measurement of Poverty", *Economic and Political Weekly*, Vol. XVI, No. 23, June. 6.

Sundram, K. et al. (1985), "The Poverty Problem", *Seminar* No. 305, Annual Number, January.

Sundram, K. (1986), *Economic Growth and Endemic Poverty in India*, Centre for Policy Research, New Delhi.

Sundram, K. and Tendulkar, S.D. (1986), "Towards an Explanation of Inter-Regional Variations in Poverty and Unemployment in Rural India", Delhi School of Economics, Working Paper No. 237.

Sundram, K. and Tendulkar, S.D. (1983), "Poverty in the Mid Term Appraisal", *Economic and Political Weekly*, Vol. XIII, November 5-12, pp. 1928 - 35.

Tendulkar, S.D. (1987), "Economic Inequalities and Poverty in India: An Interpretative Overview", *Development Process of Indian Economy*, edited by P R Brahmanda and V R Panchamukhi, Ch. 5, Himalaya Publishing House.

Thakur, D.S., *Poverty, Inequality and Unemployment in Rural India*, B R Publishing Corporation, Delhi.

Thakur, D.S. (1985), "Measurement of Inequality and Poverty in the Hilly Agrarian Economy of Himachal Pradesh—A Positive Approach", *Artha-Viskas,* January December.

Thimmiah, G. (1985), *Inequality and Poverty*, Himalaya Publishing House, Bombay, 1985.

Townsend, P. (ed.), (1970), *The Concept of Poverty*, (ed.) Heinemann, London.

Vaidyanathan, A. (1974), "Some Aspects of Inequalities in Living Standards in Rural India" In T.N. Srinivasan, and P.K. Badhan (ed.) *Poverty and Income Distribution in India*, Statistical Publishing Society, Calcutta.

Vaidyanathan, A. (1986), "On the Validity of NSS Consumption Data", *Economic and Political Weekly*, Vol. XXI, No. 6.

Visaria, Pravin (1980), "Poverty and Unemployment in India," *Indian Journal of Agriculture Economics*, Vol,

35, No. 3, July - September.

Visaria, Pravin (1992), "Data Base on poverty In India: An Exploration" In Kadekodi, G.K. and G.V.S.N Murthy (eds). *Poverty in India - Database Issues*, Vikas Publishing House, New Delhi.

Wall, D., Van, D. E. (1981), "Pollution Growth and Poverty: Another Look at the Indian Times Series Data", *Journal of Development Studies*, Vol. 21, No. 3, pp. 429-439.

Wedderburn, Dorothy (ed.) (1974), *Poverty, Inequality and Class Structure*, Cambridge University Press.

Zaidi, N.A. (1985), "Has IRDP Helped Alleviate Poverty", *Yojana*, Oct. 1-15.

Index

G

H

I

J

K

L

M

N

O

□□□